SRI AUROBINDO

THE HOUR OF GOD

SRI AUROBINDO ASHRAM
PONDICHERRY

First edition 1959
Sixth edition 2018
Second impression 2024

Rs 65
ISBN 978-93-5210-167-2

Published by Sri Aurobindo Ashram Publication Department
Pondicherry 605 002
Web https://www.sabda.in

Printed at Sri Aurobindo Ashram Press, Pondicherry
PRINTED IN INDIA

Publisher's Note

The Hour of God consists of short prose pieces written between 1910 and 1940 and published posthumously. Those selected for inclusion in this collection satisfy three further criteria. These are: (1) full development — writings more in the nature of notes than of essays have been excluded; (2) completeness — incomplete drafts and fragments have been excluded; (3) clarity of manuscript — writings that present unusual difficulties of transcription have been excluded.

The texts of all pieces published in the present volume have been checked against Sri Aurobindo's handwritten manuscripts.

Details about the texts will be found in notes at the end of the volume. Sanskrit words printed in Devanagari script are defined in these notes. Transliterated Sanskrit words are defined in a separate glossary.

Contents

Section One
The Hour of God

The Hour of God

There are moments when the Spirit moves among men and the breath of the Lord is abroad upon the waters of our being; there are others when it retires and men are left to act in the strength or the weakness of their own egoism. The first are periods when even a little effort produces great results and changes destiny; the second are spaces of time when much labour goes to the making of a little result. It is true that the latter may prepare the former, may be the little smoke of sacrifice going up to heaven which calls down the rain of God's bounty. Unhappy is the man or the nation which, when the divine moment arrives, is found sleeping or unprepared to use it, because the lamp has not been kept trimmed for the welcome and the ears are sealed to the call. But thrice woe to them who are strong and ready, yet waste the force or misuse the moment; for them is irreparable loss or a great destruction.

In the hour of God cleanse thy soul of all self-deceit and hypocrisy and vain self-flattering that thou mayst look straight into thy spirit and hear that which summons it. All insincerity of nature, once thy defence against the eye of the Master and the light of the ideal, becomes now a gap in thy armour and invites the blow. Even if thou conquer for the moment, it is the worse for thee, for the blow shall come afterwards and cast thee down in the midst of thy triumph. But being pure cast aside all fear; for the hour is often terrible, a fire and a whirlwind and a tempest, a treading of the winepress of the wrath of God; but he who can stand up in it on the truth of his purpose is he who shall stand; even though he fall, he shall rise again, even though he seem to pass on the wings of the wind, he shall return. Nor let worldly prudence whisper too closely in thy ear; for it is the hour of the unexpected, the incalculable, the immeasurable. Mete not the power of the Breath by thy petty instruments, but trust and go forward.

But most keep thy soul clear, even if for a while, of the clamour of the ego. Then shall a fire march before thee in the night and the storm be thy helper and thy flag shall wave on the highest height of the greatness that was to be conquered.

The Law of the Way

First be sure of the call and of thy soul's answer. For if the call is not true, not the touch of God's powers or the voice of his messengers, but the lure of thy ego, the end of thy endeavour will be a poor spiritual fiasco or else a deep disaster.

And if not the soul's fervour, but only the mind's assent or interest replies to the divine summons or only the lower life's desire clutches at some side attraction of the fruits of Yoga-power or Yoga-pleasure or only a transient emotion leaps like an unsteady flame moved by the intensity of the Voice or its sweetness or grandeur, then too there can be little surety for thee in the difficult path of Yoga.

The outer instruments of mortal man have no force to carry him through the severe ardours of this spiritual journey and Titanic inner battle or to meet its terrible or obstinate ordeals or nerve him to face and overcome its subtle and formidable dangers. Only his spirit's august and steadfast will and the quenchless fire of his soul's invincible ardour are sufficient for this difficult transformation and this high improbable endeavour.

Imagine not the way is easy; the way is long, arduous, dangerous, difficult. At every step is an ambush, at every turn a pitfall. A thousand seen or unseen enemies will start up against thee, terrible in subtlety against thy ignorance, formidable in power against thy weakness.

And when with pain thou hast destroyed them, other thousands will surge up to take their place. Hell will vomit its hordes to oppose thee and enring and wound and menace; Heaven will meet thee with its pitiless tests and its cold luminous denials. Thou shalt find thyself alone in thy anguish, the demons furious in thy path, the Gods unwilling above thee. Ancient and powerful, cruel, unvanquished and close and innumerable are the dark and dreadful Powers that profit by the reign of Night and Ignorance and would have no change and are hostile. Aloof, slow to arrive, far-off and few and brief in their visits are the Bright Ones who are willing or permitted to succour. Each step forward is a battle. There are precipitous descents, there are unending ascensions and ever higher peaks upon peaks to conquer. Each plateau climbed is but a stage on the way and reveals endless heights beyond it. Each victory thou thinkest the last triumphant struggle proves to be but the prelude to a hundred fierce and perilous battles... But thou sayest God's hand will be with me and the Divine Mother near with her gracious smile of succour? And thou knowest not then that God's grace is more difficult to have or to keep than the nectar of the Immortals or Kuvera's priceless treasures? Ask of His chosen and they will tell thee how often the Eternal has covered his face from them, how often he has withdrawn from them behind his mysterious veil and they have found themselves alone in the grip of Hell, solitary in the horror of the darkness, naked and defenceless in the anguish of the battle. And if his presence is felt behind the veil, yet is it like the winter sun behind clouds and saves not from the rain and snow and the calamitous storm and the harsh wind and the bitter cold and the grey of a sorrowful atmosphere and the dun weary dullness. Doubtless the help is there even when it seems to be withdrawn, but still is there the appearance of total night with no sun to come and no star of hope to pierce the blackness. Beautiful is the face of the Divine Mother, but she too can be hard and terrible. Nay, then, is immortality a plaything to be given lightly to a child or the divine life a prize without effort or the crown for a weakling? Strive rightly and thou shalt have; trust and thy trust shall in the end be justified; but the dread Law of the Way is there and none can abrogate it.

The Divine Superman

This is thy work and the aim of thy being and that for which thou art here, to become the divine superman and a perfect vessel of the Godhead. All else that thou hast to do, is only a making thyself ready or a joy by the way or a fall from thy purpose. But the goal is this and the purpose is this and not in power of the way and the joy by the way but in the joy of the goal is the greatness and the delight of thy being. The joy of the way is because that which is drawing thee is also with thee on thy path and the power to climb was given thee that thou mightest mount to thy own summits.

If thou hast a duty, this is thy duty; if thou ask what shall be thy aim, let this be thy aim; if thou demand pleasure, there is no greater joy, for all other joy is broken or limited, the joy of a dream or the joy of a sleep or the joy of self-forgetting. But this is the joy of thy whole being. For if thou say what is my being, this is thy being, the Divine, and all else is only its broken or its perverse appearance. If thou seek the Truth, this is the Truth. Place it before thee and in all things be faithful to it.

It has been well said by one who saw but through a veil and mistook the veil for the face, that thy aim is to become thyself; and he said well again that the nature of man is to transcend himself. This is indeed his nature and that is indeed the divine aim of his self-transcending.

What then is the self that thou hast to transcend

and what is the self that thou hast to become? For it is here that thou shouldst make no error; for this error, not to know thyself, is the fountain of all thy grief and the cause of all thy stumbling.

That which thou hast to transcend is the self that thou appearest to be, and that is man as thou knowest him, the apparent Purusha. And what is this man? He is a mental being enslaved to life and matter; and where he is not enslaved to life and matter, he is the slave of his mind. But this is a great and heavy servitude; for to be the slave of mind is to be the slave of the false, the limited and the apparent. The self that thou hast to become, is the self that thou art within behind the veil of mind and life and matter. It is to be the spiritual, the divine, the superman, the real Purusha. For that which is above the mental being, is the superman. It is to be the master of thy mind, thy life and thy body; it is to be a king over Nature of whom thou art now the tool, lifted above her who now has thee under her feet. It is to be free and not a slave, to be one and not divided, to be immortal and not obscured by death, to be full of light and not darkened, to be full of bliss and not the sport of grief and suffering, to be uplifted into power and not cast down into weakness. It is to live in the Infinite and possess the finite. It is to live in God and be one with him in his being. To become thyself is to be this and all that flows from it.

Be free in thyself, and therefore free in thy mind, free in thy life and thy body. For the Spirit is freedom.

Be one with God and all beings; live in thyself and

not in thy little ego. For the Spirit is unity.

Be thyself, immortal, and put not thy faith in death; for death is not of thyself, but of thy body. For the Spirit is immortality.

To be immortal is to be infinite in being and consciousness and bliss; for the Spirit is infinite and that which is finite lives only by his infinity.

These things thou art, therefore thou canst become all this; but if thou wert not these things, then thou couldst never become them. What is within thee, that alone can be revealed in thy being. Thou appearest indeed to be other than this, but wherefore shouldst thou enslave thyself to appearances?

Rather arise, transcend thyself, become thyself. Thou art man and the whole nature of man is to become more than himself. He was the man-animal, he has become more than the animal man. He is the thinker, the craftsman, the seeker after beauty. He shall be more than the thinker, he shall be the seer of knowledge; he shall be more than the craftsman, he shall be the creator and master of his creation; he shall be more than the seeker of beauty, for he shall enjoy all beauty and all delight. Physical, he seeks for his immortal substance; vital he seeks after immortal life and the infinite power of his being; mental and partial in knowledge, he seeks after the whole light and the utter vision.

To possess these is to become the superman; for [it] is to rise out of mind into the supermind. Call it the divine mind or Knowledge or the supermind; it is the power and light of the divine will and the divine consciousness.

By the supermind the Spirit saw and created himself in the worlds, by that he lives in them and governs them. By that he is Swarat Samrat, self-ruler and all-ruler.

Supermind is superman; therefore to rise beyond mind is the condition.

To be the superman is to live the divine life, to be a god; for the gods are the powers of God. Be a power of God in humanity.

To live in the divine Being and let the consciousness and bliss, the will and knowledge of the Spirit possess thee and play with thee and through thee, this is the meaning.

This is the transfiguration of thyself on the mountain. It is to discover God in thyself and reveal him to thyself in all things. Live in his being, shine with his light, act with his power, rejoice with his bliss. Be that Fire and that Sun and that Ocean. Be that joy and that greatness and that beauty.

When thou hast done this even in part, thou hast attained to the first steps of supermanhood.

Section Two

On Yoga

Certitudes

In the deep there is a greater deep, in the heights a greater height. Sooner shall man arrive at the borders of infinity than at the fulness of his own being. For that being is infinity, is God —

I aspire to infinite force, infinite knowledge, infinite bliss. Can I attain it? Yes, but the nature of infinity is that it has no end. Say not therefore that I attain it. I become it. Only so can man attain God by becoming God.

But before attaining he can enter into relations with him. To enter into relations with God is Yoga, the highest rapture & the noblest utility. There are relations within the compass of the humanity we have developed. These are called prayer, worship, adoration, sacrifice, thought, faith, science, philosophy. There are other relations beyond our developed capacity, but within the compass of the humanity we have yet to develop. Those are the relations that are attained by the various practices we usually call Yoga.

We may not know him as God, we may know him as Nature, our Higher Self, Infinity, some ineffable goal. It was so that Buddha approached Him; so approaches him the rigid Adwaitin. He is accessible even to the Atheist. To the materialist He disguises Himself in matter. For the Nihilist he waits ambushed in the bosom of Annihilation.

ये यथा मां प्रपद्यन्ते तांस्तथैव भजाम्यहम्।

Initial Definitions and Descriptions

Yoga has four powers and objects, purity, liberty, beatitude and perfection. Whosoever has consummated these four mightinesses in the being of the transcendental, universal, lilamaya and individual God is the complete and absolute Yogin.

All manifestations of God are manifestations of the absolute Parabrahman.

The Absolute Parabrahman is unknowable to us, not because It is the nothingness of all that we are, for rather whatever we are in truth or in seeming is nothing but Parabrahman, but because It is pre-existent & supra-existent to even the highest & purest methods and the most potent & illimitable instruments of which soul in the body is capable.

In Parabrahman knowledge ceases to be knowledge and becomes an inexpressible identity. Become Parabrahman, if thou wilt and if That will suffer thee, but strive not to know It; for thou shalt not succeed with these instruments and in this body.

In reality thou art Parabrahman already and ever wast and ever will be. To become Parabrahman in any other sense, thou must depart utterly out of world manifestation and out even of world transcendence.

Why shouldst thou hunger after departure from manifestation as if the world were an evil? Has not That manifested itself in thee & in the world and art thou wiser & purer & better than the Absolute, O mind-deceived soul in the mortal? When That withdraws thee, then thy going hence is inevitable; until Its force is laid on thee, thy going is impossible, cry thy mind never so fiercely & wailingly for departure. Therefore neither desire nor shun the world, but seek the bliss & purity & freedom & greatness of God in whatsoever state or experience or environment.

So long as thou hast any desire, be it the desire of non-birth or the desire of liberation, thou canst not attain to Parabrahman. For That has no desires, neither of birth nor of non-birth, nor of world, nor of departure from world. The Absolute is unlimited by thy desire as It is inaccessible to thy knowledge.

If thou wouldst know Paratpara brahman, then know It as It chooses to manifest Itself in world and transcending it — for transcendence also is a relation to world & not the sheer Absolute, — since otherwise It is unknowable. This is the simultaneous knowing & not knowing spoken of in the Vedanta.

Of Parabrahman we should not say that "It" is world-transcendent or world-immanent or related or non-related to the world; for all these ideas of world and not-world, of transcendence and immanence and relation are expressions of thought by which mind puts its own values on the self-manifestation of Parabrahman to Its own principle of knowledge and we cannot assert any, even the highest of them to be the real reality of that which is at once all and beyond all, nothing and beyond nothing. A profound and unthinking silence is the only attitude which the soul manifested in world should adopt towards the Absolute.

We know of Parabrahman that It Is, in a way in which no object is and no state in the world, because whenever & in whatever direction we go to the farthest limits of soul-experience or thought-experience or body-experience or any essential experience whatsoever, we come to the brink of That and perceive It to be, unknowably, without any capacity of experiencing about it any farther truth whatsoever.

When thy soul retiring within from depth to depth & widening without from vastness to vastness stands in the silence of its being before an unknown & unknowable from which & towards which world is seen to exist as a thing neither materially real nor mentally real and yet not to be described as a dream or a falsehood, then know that thou art standing in the Holy of Holies, before the Veil that shall not be rent. In this mortal body thou canst not rend it, nor in any other body; nor in the state of self in body nor in the state of pure self, nor in waking nor in sleep nor in trance, nor in any state or circumstances whatsoever for thou must be beyond state before thou canst enter into the Paratpara brahman.

That is the unknown God to whom no altar can be raised and no worship offered; universe is His only altar, existence is His only worship. That we are, feel, think, act or are but do not feel, do not think, do not act is for That enough. To That, the saint is equal with the sinner, activity with inactivity, man with the mollusc, since all are equally Its manifestations. These things at least are true of the Parabrahman & Para Purusha, which is the Highest that we know & the nearest to the Absolute. But what That is behind the veil or how behind the veil It regards Itself and its manifestations is a thing no mind can assume to tell or know; and he is equally ignorant and presumptuous who raises & inscribes to It an altar or who pretends to declare the Unknown to those who know that they can know It not. Confuse not thought, bewilder not the soul of man in its forward march, but turn to the Universe & know That in this, Tad va etat, for so only & in these terms It has set itself out to be known to those who are in the universe. Be not deceived by Ignorance, be not deceived by knowledge; there is none bound & none free & none seeking freedom but only God playing at these things in the extended might of His self-conscious being, para maya, mahimanam asya, which we call the universe.

The Object of Our Yoga

The object of our Yoga is self-perfection, not self-annulment.

There are two paths set for the feet of the Yogin, withdrawal from the universe and perfection in the Universe; the first comes by asceticism, the second is effected by tapasya; the first receives us when we lose God in Existence, the second is attained when we fulfil existence in God. Let ours be the path of perfection, not of abandonment; let our aim be victory in the battle, not the escape from all conflict.

Buddha and Shankara supposed the world to be radically false and miserable; therefore escape from the world was to them the only wisdom. But this world is Brahman, the world is God, the world is Satyam, the world is Ananda; it is our misreading of the world through mental egoism that is a falsehood and our wrong relation with God in the world that is a misery. There is no other falsity and no other cause of sorrow.

God created the world in Himself through Maya; but the Vedic meaning of Maya is not illusion, it is wisdom, knowledge, capacity, wide extension in consciousness. Prajna prasrita purani. Omnipotent Wisdom created the world, it is not the organised blunder of some Infinite Dreamer; omniscient Power manifests or conceals it in Itself or Its own delight, it is not a bondage imposed by His own ignorance on the free and absolute Brahman.

If the world were Brahman's self-imposed nightmare, to awake from it would be the natural and only goal of our supreme endeavour; or if life in the world were irrevocably bound to misery, a means of escape from this bondage would be the sole secret worth discovering. But perfect truth in world-existence is possible, for God here sees all things with the eye of truth; and perfect bliss in the world is possible, for God enjoys all things with the sense of unalloyed freedom. We also can enjoy this truth and bliss, called by the Veda amritam, Immortality, if by casting away our egoistic existence into perfect unity with His being we consent to receive the divine perception and the divine freedom.

The world is a movement of God in His own being; we are the centres and knots of divine consciousness which sum up and support the processes of His movement. The world is His play with His own self-conscious delight, He who alone exists, infinite, free and perfect; we are the self-multiplications of that conscious delight, thrown out into being to be His playmates. The world is a formula, a rhythm, a symbol-system expressing God to Himself in His own consciousness, — it has no material existence but exists only in His consciousness and self-expression; we, like God, are in our inward being That which is expressed, but in our outward being terms of that formula, notes of that rhythm, symbols of that system. Let us lead forward God's movement, play out His play, work out His formula, execute His harmony, express Him through ourselves in His system. This is our joy and our self-fulfilment; to this end we who transcend & exceed the universe, have entered into universe-existence.

Perfection has to be worked out, harmony has to be accomplished. Imperfection, limitation, death, grief, ignorance, matter, are only the first terms of the formula — unintelligible till we have worked out the wider terms and reinterpreted the formulary; they are the initial discords of the musician's tuning. Out of imperfection we have to construct perfection, out of limitation to discover infinity, out of death to find immortality, out of grief to recover divine bliss, out of ignorance to rescue divine self-knowledge, out of matter to reveal Spirit. To work out this end for ourselves and for humanity is the object of our Yogic practice.

The Entire Purpose of Yoga

By Yoga we can rise out of falsehood into truth, out of weakness into force, out of pain and grief into bliss, out of bondage into freedom, out of death into immortality, out of darkness into light, out of confusion into purity, out of imperfection into perfection, out of self-division into unity, out of Maya into God. All other utilisation of Yoga is for special and fragmentary advantages not always worth pursuing. Only that which aims at possessing the fullness of God is purna Yoga; the sadhaka of the Divine Perfection is the purna Yogin.

Our aim must be to be perfect as God in His being and bliss is perfect, pure as He is pure, blissful as He is blissful, and, when we are ourselves siddha in the purna Yoga, to bring all mankind to the same divine perfection. It does not matter if for the present we fall short of our aim, so long as we give ourselves whole-heartedly to the attempt and by living constantly in it and for it move forward even two inches upon the road; even that will help to lead humanity out of the struggle and twilight in which it now dwells into the luminous joy which God intends for us. But whatever our immediate success, our unvarying aim must be to perform the whole journey and not lie down content in any wayside stage or imperfect resting place.

All Yoga which takes you entirely away from the world, is a high but narrow specialisation of divine tapasya. God in His perfection embraces everything; you also must become all-embracing.

God in His ultimate existence beyond all manifestation and all knowledge, is the Absolute Parabrahman; in relation to the world He is that which transcends all universal existence while regarding it or in turning away from it; He is that which contains and upholds the universe, He is that which becomes the universe and He is the universe & everything which it contains.

He is also Absolute and Supreme Personality playing in the universe and as the universe; in the universe He appears to be its Soul & Lord, as the universe He appears to be the motion or process of the Will of the Lord and to become all the subjective and objective results of the motion. All the states of the Brahman, the transcendent, the continent, the universal, the individual are informed & sustained by the divine Personality. He is both the Existent & the state of existence. We call the state of existence the Impersonal Brahman, the Existent the Personal Brahman. There is no difference between them except to the play of our consciousness; for every impersonal state depends upon a manifest or secret Personality and can reveal the Personality which it holds and veils and every Personality attaches to itself and can plunge itself into an impersonal existence. This they can do because Personality & Impersonality are merely different states of self-consciousness in one Absolute Being.

Philosophies & religions dispute about the priority of different aspects of God & different Yogins, Rishis & Saints have preferred this or that philosophy or religion.

Our business is not to dispute about any of them, but to realise & become all of them, not to follow after any aspect to the exclusion of the rest, but to embrace God in all His aspects and beyond aspect.

God descending into world in various forms has consummated on this earth the mental and bodily form which we call humanity.

He has manifested in the world through the play of all-governing Soul with its own formative Will or Shakti a rhythm of existence of which Matter is the lowest term and pure being the highest. Mind & Life stand upon Matter (Manas & Prana on Annam) and make the lower half of world-existence (aparardha); pure consciousness and pure bliss proceed out of pure Being (Chit and Ananda out of Sat) and make the upper half of world-existence. Pure idea (vijnana) stands as the link between the two. These seven principles or terms of existence are the basis of the sevenfold world of the Puranas (Satyaloka, Tapas, Jana, Mahar, Swar, Bhuvar & Bhur).

The lower hemisphere in this arrangement of consciousness consists of the three vyahritis of the Veda, "Bhur, Bhuvah, Swar"; they are states of consciousness in which the principles of the upper world are expressed or try to express themselves under different conditions. Pure in their own homes, they are in this foreign country subject to perverse, impure & disturbing combinations & workings. The ultimate object of life is to get rid of the perversity, impurity & disturbance & express them perfectly in these other conditions. Your life on this earth is a divine poem that you are translating into earthly language or a strain of music which you are rendering into words.

Being in Sat is one in multiplicity, one that regards its multiplicity without being lost or confused in it and multiplicity that knows itself as one without losing the power of multiple play in the universe. Under the conditions of mind, life & body, ahankara is born, the subjective or objective form of consciousness is falsely taken for self-existent being, the body for an independent reality & the ego for an independent personality; the one loses itself in us in its multiplicity & when it recovers its unity, finds it difficult, owing to the nature of mind, to preserve its play of multiplicity. Therefore when we are absorbed in world, we miss God in Himself; when we seek God, we miss Him in the world. Our business is to break down & dissolve the mental ego & get back to our divine unity without losing our power of individual & multiple existence in the universe.

Consciousness in Chit is luminous, free, illimitable & effective; that which it is aware of as Chit (Jnanashakti) it fulfils infallibly as Tapas (Kriyashakti); for Jnanashakti is only the stable & comprehensive, Kriyashakti only the motional and intensive form of one self-luminous Conscious Being. They are one power of conscious force of God (Chit-Shakti of Sat-Purusha). But in the lower hemisphere, under the conditions of mind, life & body, the luminousness becomes divided & broken up into uneven rays, the freedom trammelled by egoism and unequal forms, the effectiveness veiled by the uneven play of forces. We have, therefore, states of consciousness, non-consciousness & false consciousness, knowledge & ignorance & false knowledge, effective force & inertia and ineffective force. Our business is by renouncing our divided & unequal individual force of action & thought into the one, undivided universal Chitshakti of Kali to replace our egoistic activities by the play in our body of the universal Kali and thus exchange blindness & ignorance for knowledge and ineffective human strength for the divine effective Force.

Delight in Ananda is pure, unmixed, one & yet multitudinous. Under the conditions of mind, life & body it becomes divided, limited, confused & misdirected and owing to shocks of unequal forces & uneven distribution of Ananda subject to the duality of positive & negative movements, grief & joy, pain & pleasure. Our business is to dissolve these dualities by breaking down their cause & plunge ourselves into the ocean of divine bliss, one, multitudinous, evenly distributed (sama), which takes delight from all things & recoils painfully from none.

In brief, we have to replace dualities by unity, egoism by divine consciousness, ignorance by divine wisdom, thought by divine knowledge, weakness, struggle & effort by self-contented divine force, pain & false pleasure by divine bliss. This is called in the language of Christ bringing down the kingdom of heaven on earth, or in modern language, realising & effectuating God in the world.

Humanity is, upon earth, the form of life chosen for this human aspiration & divine accomplishment; all other forms of life either do not need it or are ordinarily incapable of it unless they change into humanity. The divine fullness is therefore the sole real aim of humanity. It has to be effected in the individual in order that it may be effected in the race.

Humanity is a mental existence in a living body; its basis is matter, its centre & instrument mind & its medium life. This is the condition of average or natural humanity.

In every human being there is concealed (avyakta) the four higher principles. Mahas, pure ideality in vijnana, is not a vyahriti but the source of the vyahritis, the bank upon which mental, vital and bodily action draw & turn its large & infinite wealth into small coin of the lower existence. Vijnana being the link between the divine state & the human animal is the door of escape for man into the supernatural or divine humanity.

Inferior mankind gravitates downward from mind towards life & body; average mankind dwells constant in mind limited by & looking towards life & body; superior mankind levitates upward either to idealised mentality or to pure idea, direct truth of knowledge & spontaneous truth of existence; supreme mankind rises to divine beatitude & from that level either goes upward to pure Sat & Parabrahman or remains to beatify its lower members & raise to divinity in itself & others this human existence.

The man who dwells in the higher or divine & now hidden hemisphere of his consciousness, having rent the veil, is the true superman and the last product of that progressive self-manifestation of God in world, Spirit out of matter, which is now called the principle of evolution.

To rise into divine existence, force, light & bliss and recast in that mould all mundane existence is the supreme aspiration of religion & the complete practical aim of Yoga. The aim is to realise God in the universe, but it cannot be done without realising God transcendent of the Universe.

Parabrahman, Mukti and Human Thought-Systems

Parabrahman is the Absolute, & because It is the Absolute, it cannot be reduced into terms of knowledge. You can know the Infinite in a way, but you cannot know the Absolute.

All things in existence or non-existence are symbols of the Absolute created in self-consciousness (Chid-Atman); by Its symbols the Absolute can be known so far as the symbols reveal or hint at it, but even the knowledge of the whole sum of symbols does not amount to real knowledge of the Absolute. You can become Parabrahman; you cannot know Parabrahman. Becoming Parabrahman means going back through self-consciousness into Parabrahman, for you already are That, only you have projected yourself forward in self-consciousness into its terms or symbols, Purusha & Prakriti through which you uphold the universe. Therefore, to become Parabrahman void of terms or symbols you must cease out of the universe.

By becoming Parabrahman void of Its self-symbols you do not become anything you are not already, nor does the universe cease to operate. It only means that God throws back out of the ocean of manifest consciousness one stream or movement of Himself into that from which all consciousness proceeded.

All who go out of universe-consciousness, do not

necessarily go into Parabrahman. Some go into undifferentiated Nature (Avyakrita Prakriti), some lose themselves in God, some pass into a dark state of non-recognition of universe, (Asat, Shunya), some into a luminous state of non-recognition of universe — Pure Undifferentiated Atman, Pure Sat or Existence-Basis of Universe, — some into a temporary state of deep sleep (sushupti) in the impersonal principles of Ananda, Chit or Sat. All these are forms of release & the ego gets from God by His Maya or Prakriti the impulse towards any one of them to which the supreme Purusha chooses to direct him. Those whom He wishes to liberate, yet keep in the world, He makes jivanmuktas or sends them out again as His vibhutis, they consenting to wear for the divine purposes a temporary veil of Avidya, which does not at all bind them and which they can rend or throw off very easily. Therefore to lust after becoming Parabrahman is a sort of luminous illusion or sattwic play of Maya; for in reality there is none bound & none free & none needing to be freed and all is only God's Lila, Parabrahman's play of manifestation. God uses this sattwic Maya in certain egos in order to draw them upwards in the line of His special purpose & for these egos it is the only right and possible path.

But the aim of our Yoga is Jivanmukti in the universe; not because we need to be freed or for any other reason, but because that is God's will in us, we have to live released in the world, not released out of the world.

The Jivanmukta has, for perfect knowledge & self-fulfilment to stand on the threshold of Parabrahman, but not to cross the threshold.

The statement he brings back from the threshold is that That is & we are That, but what That is or is not, words cannot describe, nor mind discriminate.

Parabrahman being the Absolute is indescribable by any name or definite conception. It is not Being or Non-Being, but something of which Being & Non-Being are primary symbols; not Atman or unAtman or Maya; not Personality or Impersonality; not Quality or Non-Quality; not Consciousness or Non-Consciousness; not Bliss or Non-Bliss; not Purusha or Prakriti; not god nor man nor animal; not release nor bondage; but something of which all these are primary or derivative, general or particular symbols. Still, when we say Parabrahman is not this or that, we mean that It cannot in its essentiality be limited to this or that symbol or any sum of symbols; in a sense Parabrahman is all this & all this is Parabrahman. There is nothing else which all this can be.

Parabrahman being Absolute is not subject to logic, for logic applies only to the determinate. We talk confusion if we say that the Absolute cannot manifest the determinate & therefore the universe is false or non-existent. The very nature of the Absolute is that we do not know what it is or is not, what it can do or cannot do; we have no reason to suppose that there is anything it cannot do or that its Absoluteness is limited by any kind of impotency. We experience spiritually that when we go beyond everything else we come to something Absolute; we experience spiritually that the universe is in the nature of a manifestation proceeding, as it were, from the Absolute; but all these words & phrases are merely intellectual terms trying to express the inexpressible. We must state what we see as best we can, but need not dispute what others see or state; rather we must accept & in our own system locate & account for what they have seen & stated. Our only dispute is with those who deny credit to the vision or freedom & value to the statements of others; not with those who are content with stating their own vision. A philosophical or religious system is only a statement of that arrangement of existence in universe which God has revealed to us as our status of being. It is given in order that the mind may have something to stand upon while we act in Prakriti. But our vision need not be precisely the same in arrangement as the vision of others, nor is the form of thought that suits our mentality bound to suit a mentality differently constituted. Firmness, without dogmatism, in our own system, toleration, without weakness, of all other systems should therefore be our intellectual outlook.

You will find disputants questioning your system on the ground that it is not consistent with this or that Shastra or this or that great authority, whether philosopher, saint or Avatar. Remember then that realisation & experience are alone of essential importance. What Shankara argued or Vivekananda conceived intellectually about existence or even what Ramakrishna stated from his multitudinous and varied realisation, is only of value to you so far as you [are] moved by God to accept and renew it in your own experience. The opinions of thinkers & saints & Avatars should be accepted as hints but not as fetters. What matters to you is what you have seen or what God in His universal personality or impersonally or again personally in some teacher, guru or pathfinder undertakes to show to you in the path of Yoga.

The Evolutionary Aim in Yoga

In the Katha Upanishad there occurs one of those powerful and pregnant phrases, containing a world of meaning in a point of verbal space, with which the Upanishads are thickly sown. Yogo hi prabhavapyayau. For Yoga is the beginning & ending of things. In the Puranas the meaning of the phrase is underlined & developed. By Yoga God made the world, by Yoga He will draw it into Himself in the end. But not only the original creation & final dissolution of the universe, all great changes of things, creations, evolutions, destructions are effected by the essential process of Yoga, tapasya. In this ancient view Yoga presents itself as the effective, perhaps the essential & real executive movement of Nature herself in all her processes. If this is so in the general workings of Nature, if that is to say, a divine Knowledge and a divine Will in things by putting itself into relation with objects is the true cause of all force & effectuality, the same rule should hold good in human activities. It should hold good especially of all conscious & willed processes of psychological discipline, — Yogic systems, as we call them; Yoga can really be nothing but a consummate & self-conscious natural process intended to effect rapidly objects which the ordinary natural movement works out slowly, in the tardy pace of a secular or even millennial evolution.

There is an apparent difference. The aim put before

us in Yoga is God; the aim of Nature is to effect supernature; but these two aims are of one piece & intention. God & supernature are only one the real & the other the formal aspect of the one unattainable fulfilment towards which our human march is in its ascent directed. Yoga for man is the upward working of Nature liberated from slow evolution and long relapses and self-conscious in divine or human knowledge.

God is That which is the All and yet exceeds and transcends the All; there is nothing in existence which is not God, but God is neither the sum of existence nor anything in that sum, except symbolically, in image to His own consciousness. In other words, everything that exists, separately, is a particular symbol and the whole sum of existence is a general symbol which tries to translate the untranslatable existence, God, into the terms of world-consciousness. It is intended to try, it is not intended to succeed; for the moment it succeeds, it ceases to be itself and becomes that untranslatable something from which it started, God. No symbol is intended to express God perfectly, not even the highest; but it is the privilege of the highest symbols to lose in Him their separate definiteness, cease to be symbols and become in consciousness that which is symbolised. Humanity is such a symbol or eidolon of God; we are made, to use the Biblical phrase, in His image; and by that is meant not a formal image, but the image of His being and personality; we are of the essence of His divinity and of the quality of His divinity; we are formed in the mould and bear the stamp of a divine being and a divine knowledge.

In everything that exists phenomenally, or, as I shall prefer to say, going deeper into the nature of things, symbolically, there are two parts of being, thing in itself and symbol, Self and Nature, res (thing that is) and factum (thing that is done or made), immutable being and mutable becoming, that which is supernatural to it and that which is natural. Every state of existence has some force in it which drives it to transcend itself. Matter moves towards becoming life, Life travails towards becoming Mind, Mind aspires towards becoming ideal Truth, Truth rises towards becoming divine and infinite Spirit. The reason is that every symbol, being a partial expression of God, reaches out to and seeks to become its own entire reality; it aspires to become its real self by transcending its apparent self. Thing that is made, is attracted towards thing that is, becoming towards being, the natural towards the supernatural, symbol towards thing-in-itself, Nature towards God.

The upward movement is, then, the means towards self-fulfilment in this world; but it is not imperative on all objects. For there are three conditions for all changeable existences, the upward ascension, the arrested status and the downward lapse. Nature in its lower states moves upward indeed in the mass, but seeks the final salvation for only a limited number of its individuals. It is not every form of matter that organises life although every form of matter teems with the spirit of life and is full of its urgent demand for release & self-manifestation. Not every form of life organises mind, although in all forms of life mind is there, insistent, seeking for its escape and self-expression. Nor is every mental being fitted to organise the life of ideal truth, although in every mental being, in dog & ape & worm no less than in man, the imprisoned spirit of truth & knowledge seeks for its escape and self-expression. Nature in each realised state of her building seeks first to assure the natural existence of her creatures in that state; only after this primary aim is accomplished does she seek through the best fitted of them to escape from her works, to break down what she has built and arrive at something beyond. It is not till she reaches man that she arrives at a type of being of which every individual is essentially capable of realising not only the natural but the supernatural within it; and even this is true with modifications, with qualifications. But of this it will be better to speak at greater length in another connection.

Nevertheless, it remains true that the upward movement is the master movement of Nature; arrested status is a lower fulfilment, & if perfect, a transient perfection. It is a perfection in the realms of struggle and in the style of passing forms, a fulfilment in the kingdoms of Ashanaya Mrityu, Hunger who is death, Hunger that creates & feeds upon its creations; the upward movement is that which leads up through death to immortality & realises in this earth of the body the blissful and luminous kingdom of heaven; the downward lapse is destruction, Hell, a great perdition, mahati vinashtih. These are the three gatis or final states of becoming indicated in the Gita, uttama, madhyama & adhama, highest, middle and lowest, offered to the choice of humanity. It is for each individual of us to choose. For as we choose, God shall fulfil Himself in us, towards a transient human satisfaction, a divine perfection or a decomposition of our humanity into the fruitful waste-matter of Nature.

Every nature, then, is a step towards some super-nature, — towards something natural to itself, but supernatural to that which is below. Life is supernatural to Matter, Mind supernatural to Life, Ideal Being supernatural to Mind, the Infinite Spirit supernatural to ideal being. We must, therefore, accept the supernatural as our goal; for the tendency of our nature to the super-nature just above it is a command of the World Power to be obeyed and not rebelled against & distrusted. It is here that Faith has its importance & Religion, when uncorrupted, its incalculable utility; for our natural mind seeks to dwell in its nature & is sceptical of supernature. Faith & religion were provisions of the All Wise Energy to accustom the natural & merely mental man to the promptings of the ideal soul in him which seeks even now to escape out of twilight into light, out of groping into truth, out of the senses & reasoning into vision & direct experience. The upward tendency is imposed on us & we cannot permanently resist it; at some time or another God will lay his hands on us and force us up that steep incline so difficult to our unregenerate treading. For as surely as the animal develops towards humanity & in its most flexible types attains a kind of humanity, as surely as the ape and the ant having once appeared, man was bound to follow, so surely man develops towards godhead & in his more capable types approaches nearer & nearer towards godhead, attains a kind of deity, & so surely the genius & the saint having appeared man is bound to develop in himself & out of himself the superman, the siddha purusha. For this conclusion no prophetic power or revelation is needed; it is the inevitable corollary from the previous demonstrations worked out for us in the vast laboratory of Nature.

We have to transcend Nature, to become super-Nature, but it follows from what I have said that it is by taking advantage of something still imprisoned in Nature itself, by following some line which Nature is trying to open to us that we ought to proceed. By yielding to our ordinary nature we fall away both from Nature itself and from God; by transcending Nature we at once satisfy her strongest impulse, fulfil all her possibilities and rise towards God. The human first touches the divine and then becomes the divine. But there are those who seek to kill Nature in order to become the Self. Shall we follow them? No, however great & lofty be their path, however awful & dazzling their aspiration, because it is not God's intention in humanity & therefore not our proper dharma. Let any say, if he will, that we have made the lower choice. We answer in the language of the Gita, Sreyan swadharmo viguno, Better is the law of our own being though inferior, too perilous the superior law of another's being. To obey God's will in us, is certainly more blissful, perhaps even more divine than to rise to the austere heights of the Adwaitin & the ineffable self-extinction in an indefinable Existence. For us the embrace of Krishna is enough and the glory of the all-puissant bosom of Kali. We have to transcend & possess Nature, not to kill her.

In any case, whatever may be the choice for exceptional individuals, it is a general path of supreme attainment for humanity that we are seeking, — for I am not proposing to you in Yoga an individual path unconcerned with the rest of mankind, — and here there can be no doubt or hesitation. Neither the exaggerations of spirituality nor the exaggerations of materialism are our true path. Every general movement of our humanity which seeks to deny Nature, however religious, lofty or austere, of whatever dazzling purity or ethereality, has been & will always be doomed to failure, sick disappointment, disillusionment or perversion, because it is in its nature for the mass of humanity a transient impulse of exaggeration, because it contradicts God's condition for us who set Nature there as an indispensable term for His self-fulfilment in the universe and ourselves as the supreme instruments & helpers on this earth of that divine self-fulfilment. Every movement of humanity which bids us be satisfied with our ordinary Nature, dwell upon the earth, cease to aspire to the empyrean within us and choose rather to live like the animals looking to our mortal future before us & downwards at the earth we till, not upwards to God & our ungrasped perfection, has been & will always be doomed to weariness, petrifaction & cessation or to a quick & violent supernaturalistic reaction, because this also is for the mass of men a transient impulse of exaggeration & because it contradicts God's intention in us who has entered in and dwells secret in our Nature compelling us towards Him by an obscure, instinctive & overmastering attraction. Materialistic movements are more unnatural and abnormal than ascetic and negative religions & philosophies; for these lead us upward at least, though they go too furiously fast & far for our humanity, but the materialist under the pretence of bringing us back to Nature, takes us away from her entirely. He forgets or does not see that Nature is only phenomenally Nature, but in reality she is God. The divine element in her is that which she most purely & really is; the rest is only term and condition, process and stage in her whole progressively developed revelation of the secret divinity. He forgets too that Nature is evolving not evolved & what we are now can never be the term of what we shall be hereafter. The supernatural must be by the very logic of things the end & goal of her movement.

Therefore, not to be ensnared, emmeshed and bound by Nature, and not, on the other hand, to be furious with her & destroy her, is the first thing we must learn if we are to be complete Yogins and proceed surely towards our divine perfection. All beings, even the sages, follow after their nature and what shall coercion and torture of it, avail them? Prakritim yanti bhutani, nigrahah kim karishyati? And it is all so useless! Do you feel yourself bound by her and pant for release? In her hand alone is the key which shall unlock your fetters. Does she stand between you & the Lord? She is Sita; pray to her, she will stand aside & show Him to you;

but presume not to separate Sita & Rama, to cast her out into some distant Lanca under the guard of giant self-tortures so that you may have Rama to yourself in Ayodhya. Wrestle with Kali, if you will, she loves a good wrestler; but wrestle not with her unlovingly, or in mere disgust & hate; for her displeasure is terrible and though she loves the Asuras, she destroys them. Rather go through her & under her protection, go with a right understanding of her and with a true & unfalteringWill; she will lead you on with whatever circlings, yet surely & in the wisest way, to the All-Blissful Personality & the Ineffable Presence. Nature is the Power of God Himself, leading these multitudes of beings, through the night & the desert & the tracts of the foeman to their secret & promised heritage.

Supernature, then, is in every way our aim in Yoga; being still natural to the world, to transcend Nature internally so that both internally and externally we may possess and enjoy her as free & lord, swarat and samrat; being still the symbol in a world of symbol-beings, to reach through it to that which is symbolised, to realise the symbol; being still a figure of humanity, a man among men, a living body among living bodies, manus, mental beings housed in that living matter among other embodied mental beings; being & remaining in our outward parts all this that we are apparently, yet to exceed it and become in the body what we are really in the secret self, — God, spirit, supreme & infinite being, pure Bliss of divine joy, pure Force of divine action, pure Light of divine knowledge. Our whole apparent life has only a symbolic value & is good & necessary as a becoming; but all becoming has being for its goal & fulfilment & God is the only being. To become divine in the nature of the world and in the symbol of humanity is the perfection for which we were created.

The Fullness of Yoga — In Condition

We are to exceed our human stature and become divine; but if we are to do this, we must first get God; for the human ego is the lower imperfect term of our being, God is the higher perfect term. He is the possessor of our supernature and without His permission there can be no effectual rising. The finite cannot become infinite unless it perceives its own secret infinity and is drawn by it or towards it; nor can the symbol-being, unless it glimpses, loves and pursues the Real-being in itself, overcome by its own strength the limits of its apparent nature. It is a particular becoming & is fixed in the nature of the symbol that it has become; only the touch of that which is all becomings and exceeds all becomings, can liberate it from the bondage to its own limited Nature. God is That which is the All and which exceeds the All. It is therefore only the knowledge, love and possession of God that can make us free. He who is transcendent, can alone enable us to transcend ourselves; He who is universal can alone enlarge us from our limited particular existence.

In this necessity is the justification of that great & imperishable force of Nature, which Rationalism has unjustly & irrationally despised, Religion. I speak of religion, — not of a creed, church or theology, for all these things are rather forms of religiosity than essence or even always action of religion, — but of that personal and intimate religion, a thing of temper and spirit and life, not of views & formal actions, which draws a man passionately and absorbingly to his own vision of the Supreme or his own idea of something higher than himself which he must follow or become. Without a fervent worship of the Supreme in the heart, a strong aspiration upwards to It in the will or a vehement thirst for it in the temperament, we cannot have the impulse to be other than ourselves or the force to do anything so difficult as the transcending of our own ingrained and possessing human nature. The prophets have spoken & the Avatars have descended always for the one purpose, to call us to God, to inspire us to this great call on our upward straining energies or else to prepare something in the world which will help to bring humanity nearer to the goal of its difficult ascending journey.

It may seem at first sight that there is no need for these religious terms or this religious spirit. If the aim is to become something superior to man, to evolve a superman out of ourselves, as man has been evolved out of the ape, — if that statement of the progression be indeed the truth, — the ape out of inferior animal forms, they again out of mollusc & protoplasm, jellyfish or vegetable animals, & so to the end of the series, then what need is there of anything but the training, preferably the most intelligent & scientific training of our mental, moral and physical energies till they reach a point when they are transmuted by the psychical chemistry of Nature into the coming superior type? But the problem is not so simple, in reality. There are three errors hidden at the basis of this sceptical question. We mistake the nature of the operation to be effected, we mistake the nature of the power & process that works it out, we mistake the nature of the thing that uses the power & works out the process.

Nature does not propose to man to work out a higher mental, moral and physical variation-type in the mould of the present human being, — the symbol we are; it proposes to break that general type altogether in order to advance to a new symbol being which shall be supernatural to present man as present man is to the animal below him. It is doubtful whether in the pure human mould Nature can go much farther than she has gone at present; that she can for instance produce a higher mental type than Newton, Shakespeare, Caesar or Napoleon, a higher moral type than Buddha, Christ or St Francis, a higher physical type than the Greek athlete or to give modern examples, a Sandow or a Ramamurti. She may seek to bring about a better combination of mental & moral, or of moral, mental & physical energies; but is she likely to produce anything much above the level of Confucius or Socrates? It is more probable & seems to be true that Nature seeks in this field to generalise a higher level and a better combination. Neither need we believe that, even here, her object is to bring all men to the same level; for that can only be done by levelling downwards. Nothing in Nature is free from inequalities except the forms that are the lowest and least developed. The higher the effort accomplished, the more richly endowed the organism of the species, the greater the chances of inequality. In so high and developed a natural movement as Man, equality of individual opportunity is conceivable, equality of natural powers and accomplishment is a chimera. Nor will the generalisation of powers or the increase of material make any difference to the level of natural attainment. All the accumulated discoveries & varied information of the modern scientist will not make him mentally the superior of Aristotle or Socrates; he is neither an acuter mind nor a greater mental force. All the varied activities of modern philanthropy will not produce a greater moral type than Buddha or St Francis. The invention of the motor car will not make up for the lost swiftness & endurance nor gymnastics restore the physical capacity of the Negro or the American Indian. We see therefore the limits of Nature's possibilities in the human symbol, fixed by the character of the symbol itself and recognised by her in her strivings.

It is still a question whether in these limits the chief preoccupation of Nature is the exhaustion of the possibilities of the human symbol. That is rather man's preoccupation and therefore the direction she takes when human intellect interferes with her normal progression. Left to herself & even utilising human interferences, she seems bent rather on breaking the mould, than on perfecting it, — only indeed in her more advanced individuals & more daring movements and with due regard to the safety of the general human type, but this is always her method when she wishes to advance to a fresh symbol without destroying the anterior species. The more civilised man becomes, the more she plagues him with moral abnormalities, excesses of vice & virtue and confusions of the very type of vice & virtue; the more he intellectualises, the more he insists on rationality as his utmost bourne, the more she becomes dissatisfied and clamours to him to develop rather his instincts & his intuitions; the more he strives after health & hygiene, the more she multiplies diseases & insanities of mind and body. He has triumphed over supernaturalism, he has chained her down to the material, human & rational; immediately she breaks out fiercely into unthought-of revivals and gigantic supernaturalisms. Whatever work she is intent on, she will not be baulked in that work by the limited human reason. Through all her vast being she feels the pulsation of a supernatural power, the workings & strivings of a knowledge superior to material reason. She breaks out, therefore, she compels, she insists. Everywhere we see her striving to break the mental, moral & physical type she has created & to get beyond it to some new processes as yet not clearly discerned. She attacks deliberately the sound healthfulness & equilibrium of our normal type of intellectuality, morality & physical being. She is stricken also with a mania of colossalism; colossal structures, colossal combinations, colossal heights & speeds, colossal dreams & ambitions outline themselves everywhere more or less clearly, more or less dimly. Unable as yet to do her will in the individual, she works with masses; unable in the mind, with material forms & inventions; unable in actualities, with hopes & dreams; unable to reproduce or produce Napoleons & super-Napoleons, she generalises a greater reach of human capacity from which they may hereafter emerge more easily, & meanwhile she creates instead Dreadnoughts & Super-dreadnoughts, Trusts & mammoth combines, teems with distance destroying inventions & seems eager & furious to trample to pieces the limitations of space & time she herself has created.

As if to point her finger to the thing she intends, she has accumulated the signs of this process of breaking & rebuilding in the phenomena of genius. It is now common knowledge that genius hardly appears in the human species unattended, unprepared or unaccompanied by abnormalities in the individual body, vitality & mind which contains it, — degeneration, insanity or freak in the heredity which produces it and even disturbance & supranormality in the human environment in which it occurs. The haste of a brilliant generalisation establishes on this basis the paradox that genius itself is a morbid phenomenon of insanity or degeneration. The true explanation is sufficiently clear. In order to establish genius in the human system, Nature is compelled to disturb & partially break the normality of that system, because she is introducing into it an element that is alien as it is superior to the type which it enriches. Genius is not the perfect evolution of that new & divine element; it is only a beginning or at the highest an approximation in certain directions. It works fitfully & uncertainly in the midst of an enormous mass of somewhat disordered human mentality, vital nervosity, physical animality. The thing itself is divine, it is only the undivine mould in which it works that is to a lesser or greater extent broken & ploughed up by the unassimilated force that works in it. Sometimes there is an element in the divine intruder which lays its hand on the mould & sustains it, so that it does not break at all, nor is flawed; or if there is a disturbance, it is slight and negligible. Such an element there was in Caesar, in Shakespeare, in Goethe. Sometimes also a force appears to which we can no longer apply the description of genius without being hopelessly inadequate in our terminology. Then those who have eyes to see, bow down and confess the Avatar. For it is often the work of the Avatar to typify already, partly or on the whole, what Nature has not yet effected in the mass or even in the individual, so that his passing may stamp it on the material ether in which we live.

But what is this type of which the great Mother is in labour? What birth will emerge from the cries & throes of this prolonged & mighty pregnancy? A greater type of humanity, it may be said. But in order to understand what we are saying, we must first see clearly what the humanity is which she seeks to surpass. This human symbol, this type we now are is a mental being with a mental ego, working in a vital case by mind always, but upon matter, in matter & through matter. It is limited in its higher workings by its lower instruments. Its basis of mind is egoistic, sensational & determined by experience & environment, its knowledge therefore pursues wider or narrower circles in a fixed and meagre range. Its moral temperament & action is similarly egoistic, sensational, experiential and determined by environment;

for this reason it is bound equally to sin & virtue and all attempts radically to moralise the race within the limits of its egoistic nature have been & must necessarily, in spite of particular modifications, end in general failure. It is not only a mixed but a confused type, body & vitality interfering with mind & mind both hampered by & hampering body & vitality. Its search for knowledge, founded on sense contact, is a groping like that of a man finding his way in a forest at night; it makes acquaintance with its surroundings by touching, dashing on or stumbling over them; and, although it has an uncertain light of reason given it which partially corrects this disability, yet since reason has also to start from the senses which are consistent falsifiers of values, rational knowledge is not only restricted but pursued by vast dimnesses & uncertainties even in that which it seems to itself to have grasped. It secures a few flowers of truth by rummaging in a thorny hedge of doubts & errors. The actions of the type also are a breaking through thickets, a sanguine yet tormented stumbling forward through eager failures to partial and temporary successes. Immensely superior to all else that Nature had yet effected, this type is yet so burdened with disabilities, that, if it were impossible to break its mould and go forward, there would be much justification for those pessimistic philosophies which despair of Life & see in the Will not to Live humanity's only door of escape admitting to it no other salvation. But Nature is the will of the all-Wise God and she is not working out a reduction of the world to absurdity. She knows her goal, she knows that man as he is at present is only a transitional type; and so far as she can consistently with the survival of the type, she presses forward to what she has seen in God's eternal knowledge as standing beyond. From this ego, she moves towards a universal consciousness, from this limitation to a free movement in infinity, from this twilit & groping mind to the direct sunlit vision of things, from this conflict without issue between vice & virtue to a walking that keeps spontaneously to a God-appointed path, from this broken & grief-besieged action to a joyous & free activity, from this confused strife of our members to a purified, unentangled and harmonious combination, from this materialised mentality to an idealised & illuminated life, body & mind, from the symbol to reality, from man separated from God to man in God & God in man. In brief, as she has aspired successfully from matter to life, from life to mind & mental ego, so she aspires & with a fated success to an element beyond mind, the vijnana of the Hindus, the self-luminous idea or Truth-self now concealed & superconscious in man and the world, as life was always concealed in matter and mind in life. What this vijnana is, we have yet to see, but through it she knows she can lay firm hold on that highest term of all which is the reality of all symbols, in Spirit, in Sachchidananda.

The aim of Nature is also the aim of Yoga. Yoga, like Nature at its summit, seeks to break this mould of ego, this mould of mentalised life body and materialised mind, in order to achieve ideal action, ideal truth and infinite freedom in our spiritual being. To effect so enormous an end great and dangerous processes have to be used. Those who have been eager on this road or have opened up new paths towards the goal, have had to affront as a possibility frequently realised loss of reason, loss of life & health or dissolution of the moral being. They are not to be pitied or scorned even when they succumb; rather are they martyrs for humanity's progress, far more than the lost navigator or the scientist slain by the dangers of his investigation. They prepare consciently the highest possible achievement towards which the rest of humanity instinctively & unconsciously moves. We may even say that Yoga is the appointed means Nature holds in reserve for the accomplishment of her end, when she has finished her long labour of evolving at least a part of humanity temperamentally equal to the effort and intellectually, morally & physically prepared for success. Nature moves toward supernature, Yoga moves towards God; the world-impulse & the human aspiration are one movement and the same journey.

Nature

If this is the nature of the operation to be effected, not a perfection of the present human mould but a breaking of it to proceed to a higher type, what then is the power & process that works it out? What is this Nature of which we speak so fluently?[1] We habitually talk of it as if it were something mighty & conscious that lives and plans; we credit it with an aim, with wisdom to pursue that aim and with power to effect what it pursues. Are we justified in our language by the actualities of the universe or is this merely our inveterate habit of applying human figures to non-human things and the workings of intelligence to non-intelligent processes which come right because they must and not because they will and produce this magnificent ordered universe by some dumb blind and brute necessity inconceivable in its origin & nature to intelligent beings? If so, this blind brute force has produced something higher than itself, something which did not exist preconceived in its bosom or in any way belong to it. We cannot understand

[1] *The following sentence was written at the beginning of this essay during revision. It was not worked into the text, and so is given here as a footnote:*

Nature is Force of Consciousness in infinite Being. The opinion that sees a mechanical world in which consciousness is only an exceptional figure of things, is a hasty conclusion drawn from imperfect data.

what being & Nature are, not because we are as yet too small and limited, but because we are too much above being & Nature. Our intelligence is a luminous freak in a darkness from which it was impossibly produced, since nothing in that darkness justified itself as a cause of its creation. Unless mind was inherent in brute matter, — & in that case matter is only apparently brute, — it was impossible for matter to produce mind. But since this leads us to an impossibility, it cannot be the truth. We must suppose then, if matter is brute, that mind is also brute. Intelligence is an illusion; there is nothing but a shock of material impacts creating vibrations & reactions of matter which translate themselves into the phenomena of intelligence. Knowledge is only a relation of matter with matter, and is intrinsically neither different nor superior to the hurtling of atoms against each other or the physical collision of two bulls in a meadow. The material agents involved & phenomenon produced are different & therefore we do not call the recoil of one horned forehead from another an act of knowledge or intelligence, but the thing that has happened is intrinsically the same. Intelligence is itself inert & mechanical & merely the physiological result of a physiological movement & has nothing in it psychical or mental in the time-honoured sense of the words soul and mind. This is the view of modern scientific rationalism, — put indeed in other language than the scientist's, put so as to bring out its logical consequences & implications, but still effectively the modern account of the universe.

In that account the nature of a thing consists of

its composition, the properties contained in that composition and the laws of working determined by those properties; as for [example] iron is composed of certain elementary substances, possesses as a consequence of its composition certain properties, such as hardness etc. and under given circumstances will act in a given manner as the result of its properties. Applying this analysis on a larger scale we see the universe as the composition of certain brute forces working in certain material substances, possessed in itself and in those substances of certain primary & secondary, general & particular properties and working as a result by certain invariable tendencies & fixed processes which we call by a human figure Nature's Laws. This is Nature. When searchingly analysed she is found to be a play of two entities, Force & Matter; but these two, if the unitarian view of the universe is correct, will some day be proved to be only one entity, either only Matter or only Force.

Even if we accept this modern view of the universe, which, it is not at all dangerous to prophesy, will have disappeared in the course of a century into a larger synthesis, there is still something to be said about the presence or absence of intelligence in Nature. In what after all does intelligence consist, what are its composition, properties, laws? What in its circumstances is human intelligence, the only kind of intelligence which we are in a position to study from within & therefore understand? It is marked by three qualities or processes, the power & process of adaptation towards an end, the power & process of discrimination between the impacts on its senses

& the power & process of mentally conscious comprehension. Human intelligence is, to put it briefly, teleological, discriminative and mentally conscious. About other than human beings, about animals, trees, metals, forces, we can say nothing from inside, we can only infer the absence or presence of these elements of consciousness from the evidence collected by an external observation. We cannot positively say, having no internal evidence, that the tree is not a mind imprisoned in matter and unable to express itself in the media it has at its disposal; we cannot say that it does not suffer the reactions of pleasure and pain; but from the external evidence we infer to the contrary. Our negative conclusion is probable, it is not certain. It may be itself negatived in the future march of knowledge. But still, taking the evidence as it stands, what are the facts we actually arrive at in this comparison of intelligent & non-intelligent Nature?

First, Nature possesses in a far higher degree than man the teleological faculty & process. To place an aim before one, to combine, adapt, modify, unify, vary means & processes in order to attain that end, to struggle against and overcome difficulties, to devise means to circumvent difficulties when they cannot be overcome, this is one of the noblest & divinest parts of human intelligence. But its action in man is only a speciality of its universal action in Nature. She works it out in man partly through the reason, in animals with very little & rudimentary reason, mainly through instinct, memory, impulse & sensation, in plants & other objects with very little & rudimentary reason, mainly through impulse & mechanical or, as we call it, involuntary action. But throughout there is the end & the adaptation to the end, & throughout the same basic means are used; for in man also it is only for a selection of his ends & processes that the reason is used; for the greater part she uses the animal means, memory, impulse, sensation, instinct, — instincts differently directed, less decisive & more general than the animal instincts but still in the end & for their purpose as sure; & for yet another part she uses the same merely mechanical impulse & involuntary action precisely as in her mistermed inanimate forms of existence. Let us not say that the prodigality of Nature, her squandering of materials, her frequent failure, her apparent freaks and gambollings are signs of purposelessness and absence of intelligence. Man with his reason is guilty of the same laches and wanderings. But neither Man nor Nature is therefore purposeless or unintelligent. It is Nature who compels Man himself to be other than too strenuously utilitarian, for she knows better than the economist & the utilitarian philosopher. She is an universal intelligence & she has to attend, not only in the sum, but in each detail, to the universal as well as to the particular effect; she has to work out each detail with her eye on the group and not only on the group but the whole kind & not only on the whole kind but the whole world of species. Man, a particular intelligence limited by his reason, is incapable of this largeness; he puts his particular ends in the forefront and neither sees where absorption in them hurts his general well being nor can divine where they clash with the universal purpose. Her failures have an utility — we shall see before long how great an utility; her freaks have a hidden seriousness. And yet above all she remembers that beyond all formal ends, her one great object is the working out of universal delight founded on arrangement as a means, but exceeding its means. Towards that she moves; she takes delight on the way, she takes delight in the work, she takes delight, too, beyond the work.

But in all this we anticipate, we speak as if Nature were self-conscious; what we have arrived at is that Nature is teleological, more widely than man, more perfectly than man, & man himself is only teleological because of that in Nature & by the same elementary means & processes as the animal & the plant, though with additions of fresh means peculiar to mind. This, it may be said, does not constitute Intelligence, — for intelligence is not only teleological, but discriminative & mentally conscious. Mechanical discrimination, Nature certainly possesses in the highest degree; without it her teleological processes would be impossible. The tendril growing straight through the air comes into contact with a rope, a stick, the stalk of a plant; immediately it seizes it as with a finger, changes its straight growth for a curled & compressive movement, & winds itself round & round the support. What induces the change? what makes it discriminate the presence of a support & the possibility of this new movement? It is the instinct of the tendril and differs in no way, intrinsically, from the instinct of the newborn pup seizing at once on its mother's teats or the instinct of a man in his more mechanical needs

& actions. We see the moon-lotus open its petals to the moon, close them to the touch of the day. In what does this discriminative movement differ from the motion of the hand leaping back from the touch of a flame, or from the recoiling movement of disgust & displeasure in the nerves from an abhorrent sight or from the recoiling movement of denial & uncongeniality in the mind from a distasteful idea or opinion? Intrinsically, there seems to be no difference; but there is a difference in circumstance. One is not attended with mental self-consciousness, the others are attended with this supremely important element. We think falsely that there is no will in the action of the tendril and the lotus, and no discrimination. There is a will, but not mentalised will; there is discrimination but not mentalised discrimination. It is mechanical, we say, — but do we understand what we mean when we say it, — & we give other names, calling will force, discrimination a natural reaction or an organic tendency. These names are only various masks concealing an intrinsic identity.

Even if we could go no farther, we should have gained an enormous step; for we have already the conception of the thing we call Nature as possessing, containing or identical with a great Force of Will placing before itself a vast end & a million complexly related incidental ends, working them out by contrivance, adaptation, arrangement, device, using an unfailing discrimination & vastly fulfilling its complex work. Of this great Force human intelligence would only be a limited and inferior movement, guided and used by it, serving its ends even when it seems to combat its ends. We may deny Intelligence to such a Power, because it does not give signs of mental consciousness & does not in every part of its works use a human or mental intelligence; but our objection is only a metaphysical distinction. Practically, looking out on life & not in upon abstract thought, we can, if we admit this conception, rely on it that the workings of this unintelligent discrimination will be the same as if they were the workings of a universal Intelligence & the aim & means of the mechanical will the aims & means which would be chosen by an Almighty Wisdom. But if we arrive at this certainty, does not Reason itself demand of us that we should admit in Nature or behind it a universal Intelligence and an Almighty Wisdom? If the results are such as these powers would create, must we not admit the presence of these powers as the cause? Which is the truer Rationalism, to admit that the works of Intelligence are produced by Intelligence or to assert that they are produced by a blind Machine unconsciously working out perfection? to admit that the emergence of overt intelligence in humanity is due to the specialised function of a secret intelligence in the universe or to assert that it is the product of a Force to which the very principle of Intelligence is absent? To justify the paradox by saying that things are worked out in a particular way because it is their nature to be worked out in that way, is to play the fool with reason; for it does not carry us an inch beyond the mere fact that they are so worked out, one knows not why.

The true reason for the modern reluctance to admit

that Nature has intelligence & wisdom or is intelligence & wisdom, is the constant association in the human mind of these things with mentally self-conscious personality. Intelligence, we think, presupposes someone who is intelligent, an ego who possesses & uses this intelligence. An examination of human consciousness shows that this association is an error. Intelligence possesses us, not we intelligence; intelligence uses us, not we intelligence. The mental ego in man is a creation & instrument of intelligence and intelligence itself is a force of Nature manifesting itself in a rudimentary or advanced state in all animal life. This objection, therefore, vanishes. Not only so, but Science herself by putting the ego in its right place as a product of mind has shown that Intelligence is not a human possession but a force of Nature & therefore an attribute of Nature, a manifestation of the universal Force.

The question remains, is it a fundamental & omnipresent attribute or only a development manifested in a select minority of her works? Here again, the difficulty is that we associate intelligence with an organised mental consciousness. But let us look at & interrogate the facts which Science has brought into our ken. We will glance at only one of them, the fly catching plant of America. Here is a vegetable organism which has hunger, — shall we say, an unconscious hunger, which needs animal food, which sets a trap for it, as the spider sets it, which feels the moment the victim touches the trap, which immediately closes & seizes the prey, eats & digests it & lies in wait for more. These motions are exactly the motions of the spider's mental intelligence altered & conditioned only by the comparative immobility of the plant & confined only, so far as we can observe, to the management of this supreme vital need & its satisfaction. Why should we attribute mental intelligence to the spider & none to the plant? Granted that it is rudimentary, organised only for special purposes, still it would seem to be the same natural Force at work in the spider & plant, intelligently devising means to an end & superintending the conduct of the device. If there is no mind in the plant, then, irresistibly, mental intelligence & mechanical intelligence are one & the same thing in essence, & the tendril embracing its prop, the plant catching its prey & the spider seizing its victim are all forms of one Force of action, which we may decline to call Intelligence if we will, but which is obviously the same thing as Intelligence. The difference is between Intelligence organised as mind, & Intelligence not organised but working with a broad elementary purity more unerring, in a way, than the action of mind. In the light of these facts the conception of Nature as infinite teleological & discriminative Force of Intelligence unorganised & impersonal because superior to organisation & personality becomes the supreme probability, the mechanical theory is only a possibility. In the absence of certainties Reason demands that we should accept the probable in preference to the possible and a harmonious & natural in preference to a violent and paradoxical explanation.

But is it certain that in this Intelligence & its works Mind is a speciality and Personality — as distinguished from mental ego — is entirely absent except as an efflorescence & convenience of Mind? We think so, because we suppose that where there are no animal signs of consciousness, there consciousness cannot and does not exist. This also may be an assumption. We must remember that we know nothing of the tree & the stone except its exterior signs of life or quiescence; our internal knowledge is confined to the phenomena of human psychology. But even in this limited sphere there is much that should make us think very deeply and pause very long before we hasten to rash negative assertions. A man sleeps, dreamlessly, he thinks; but we know that all the time consciousness is at work within him, dreaming, always dreaming; of his body & its surroundings he knows nothing, yet that body is of itself conducting all the necessary operations of life. In the man stunned or in trance there is the same phenomenon of a divided being, consciousness mentally active within apart from the body which is mentally even as the tree & the stone, but vitally active & functioning like the tree. Catalepsy presents a still more curious phenomenon of a body dead & inert like the stone, not even vitally active like the tree, but a mind perfectly aware of itself, its medium & its surroundings, though no longer in active possession of the medium and therefore no longer able to act materially on its surroundings. In face of these examples how can we assert that there is no life in the stone, no mind in stone or tree? The premise of the syllogism by which science denies mind to the tree or life to the stone, viz that where there is no outward sign of life or conscious mentality, life & mentality do not exist, is proven to be false. The possibility, even a certain probability presents itself, — in view of the unity of Nature & the omnipresent intelligence in her works, that the tree & the stone are in their totality just such a divided being, a form not yet penetrated & possessed by conscious mind, a conscious intelligence within dreaming in itself or, like the cataleptic, aware of its surroundings, but because not yet possessed of its medium (the intelligence in the cataleptic is temporarily dispossessed) unable to show any sign of life or of mentality or to act aggressively on its surroundings.

We do not need to stop at this imperfect probability, for the latest researches of psychology make it almost overwhelming in its insistence & next door to the actual proof. We now know that within men there is a dream self or sleep self other than the waking consciousness, active in the stunned, the drugged, the hypnotised, the sleeping, which knows what the waking mind does not know, understands what the waking mind does not understand, remembers accurately what the waking mind has not even taken the trouble to notice. Who is this apparent sleeper in the waking, this waker in the sleeping in comparison with whose comprehensive attentiveness & perfect observation, memory and intelligence our waking consciousness is only a fragmentary & hasty dream? Mark this capital point that this more perfect consciousness within us is not the product of evolution, — nowhere in the evolved & waking world is there such a being who remembers & repeats automatically the sounds of a foreign language which is unnoticed jabbering to the instructed mind, solves spontaneously problems from which the instructed mind has retired baffled & weary, notices everything, understands everything, recalls everything. Therefore this consciousness within is independent of evolution and, consequently, we may presume, anterior to evolution. Esha supteshu jagarti, says the Katha Upanishad, This is the Waker in all who sleep.

This new psychological research is only in its infancy & cannot tell us what this secret consciousness is, but the knowledge gained by Yoga enables us to assert positively that this is the complete mental being within who guides life & body, manomayah pranashariraneta. He it is who conducts our evolution & awakes mind out of life & is more & more getting possession of this vitalised human body, his medium & instrument, so that it may become what it is not now, a perfect instrument of mentality. In the stone he also is and in the tree, in those sleepers also there is one who wakes; but he has not in those forms got possession yet of the instrument for the purposes of mind; he can only use them for the purposes of vitality in its growth or in its active functioning.

We see, therefore, modern psychology, although it still gets away from the only rational & logical conclusion possible on its data, marching inevitably & under the sheer compulsion of facts to the very truths arrived at thousands of years ago by the ancient Rishis. How did they arrive at them? Not by speculation, as the scholars vainly imagine, but by Yoga. For the great stumbling block that has stood in the way of Science is its inability to get inside its object, the necessity under which it labours of building on inferences from external study, — & all its desperate & cruel attempts to make up the deficiency by vivisection or other ruthless experiments cannot remedy the defect. Yoga enables us to get inside the object by dissolving the artificial barriers of the bodily experience & the mental ego-sense in the observer. It takes us out of the little hold of personal experience and casts us into the great universal currents; takes us out of the personal mind sheath & makes [us] one with universal self and universal mind. Therefore were the ancient Rishis able to see what now we are beginning again to glimpse dimly that not only is Nature herself an infinite teleological and discriminative impersonal Force of Intelligence or Consciousness, prajna prasrita purani,[2] but that God dwells within & over Nature as infinite universal Personality, universal in the universe, individualised as well as universal in the particular form, or self-consciousness who perceives, enjoys & conducts to their end its vast & complex workings. Not only is there Prakriti; there is also Purusha.

So far, then, we succeed in forming some idea of the great force which is to work out our emergence from our nature to our supernature. It is a force of Conscious Being manifesting itself in forms & movements & working out exactly as it is guided, from stage to stage, the predetermined progress of our becoming & the Will of God in the world.

[2] Intelligent Consciousness that went forth in the beginning.
— Swetaswatara Upanishad

Maya

The world exists as symbol of Brahman; but the mind creates or accepts false values of things and takes symbol for essential reality. This is ignorance or cosmic illusion, the mistake of the mind & senses, from which the Magician Himself, Master of the Illusion, is calling on us to escape. This false valuation of the world is the Maya of the Gita and can be surmounted without abandoning either action or world-existence. But in addition, the whole of universal existence is in this sense an illusion of Maya that it is not an unchanging transcendent and final reality of things but only a symbolical reality; it is a valuation of the reality of Brahman in the terms of cosmic consciousness. All these objects we see or are mentally aware of as objectively existing, are only forms of consciousness. They are the thing-in-itself turned first into terms & ideas born of a movement or rhythmic process of consciousness and then objectivised, in consciousness itself and not really external to it. They have therefore a fixed conventional reality, but not an eternally durable essential reality; they are symbols, not altogether the thing symbolised, means of knowledge, not altogether the thing known. To look at it from another point of view Existence or Brahman has two fundamental states of consciousness, cosmic consciousness and transcendental consciousness. To cosmic consciousness the world is real as a direct first term expressing the inexpressible; to transcendental consciousness the world is only a secondary & indirect term expressing the inexpressible. When I have the cosmic consciousness, I see the world as my Self manifested; in transcendental consciousness I see the world not as the manifestation of my Self but as a manifestation of something I choose to be to my Self-consciousness. It is a conventional term expressing me which does not bind me; I could dissolve it and express myself otherwise. It is a vocable of a particular language expressing something in speech or writing which could be equally well expressed by quite another vocable in another language. I say tiger in English; I might equally have spoken Sanscrit & used the word shardula; it would have made no difference to the tiger or to myself, but only to my play with the symbols of speech and thought. So it is with Brahman & the universe, the Thing in itself and its symbols with their fixed conventional values, some of which are relative to the general consciousness & some to the individual consciousness of the symbol-being. Matter, Mind, Life for instance are general symbols with a fixed general value to God in His cosmic consciousness; but they have a different individual value, make a different impression or represent themselves differently, as we say, to myself, to the ant or to the god and angel. This perception of the purely conventional value of form & name in the Universe is expressed in metaphysics by the formula that the world is a creation of Para Maya or supreme Cosmic Illusion.

It does not follow that the world is unreal or has no

existence worth the name. None of the ancient Scriptures of Hinduism affirms the unreality of the world, nor is it a logical consequence of the great but remote and difficult truth words are so inadequate to express. We must remember that all these terms, Maya, illusion, dream, unreality, relative reality, conventional value, are merely verbal figures and must not be pressed with a too literal scholastic or logical insistence. They are like the paintbrush hurled by the painter at his picture in desperation at not arriving at the effect he wanted; they are stones thrown at the truth, not the truth itself. We shall see this clearly enough when we come to look at the Cosmos from quite another standpoint, — the standpoint not of Maya, but Lila.[1] But certain great metaphysical minds, not perceiving sufficiently that words like everything else have only conventional values and are symbols of a truth which is in itself inexpressible, have drawn from the ideas suggested by these words, the most rigorous and concrete conclusions. They have condemned the whole world as a miserable & lying dream, all the more hateful & profitless for a certain element of ineffugable reality which the more clearsighted part of their minds was compelled to realise & partially to admit. The truth in their premises has made their doctrines a mighty instrument for the liberation of great & austere souls, the error in their conclusion has afflicted humanity with

[1] Illusion is itself an illusion. That which seems to the soul escaping from ignorance to be Maya, an illusion or dream, is seen by the soul already free to be Lila of God and the spirit's play.

the vain & barren gospel of the vanity not only of false mundane existence, but of all mundane existence. In the extreme forms of this view both nature & supernature, man & God are lies of consciousness, myths of a cosmic dream & not worth accepting. Amelioration is a chimera, divinity a lure and only absorption in a transmundane impersonal existence worth pursuing. The worshippers of God, the seekers after human perfection, those who would raise humanity from nature to supernature, find in their path two great stumbling blocks, on one side, the lower trend of Nature to persist in its past gains which represents itself in the besotted naturalism of the practical man & the worldling and on the other, this grand overshooting of the mark represented not only by the world-fleeing ascetic, who is after all, within his rights, but by the depressing pessimism of the ignorant who mean neither to flee the world, nor, if they did, could rise to the real grandeur of asceticism, but are still imbued intellectually & overshadowed in temperament by these high & fatal doctrines. A better day will dawn for India when the shadow is lifted and the Indian mental consciousness without renouncing the truth of Maya, perceives that it is only a partial explanation of existence. Mundane existence is not indispensable either to God's being or to God's bliss, but it is not therefore a vanity; nor is a liberated mundane existence — liberated in God — either a vain or a false existence.

The ordinary doctrine of Maya is not a simple truth, but proceeds upon three distinct spiritual perceptions. The first & highest is this supreme perception that the world is a mass of consciousness-symbols, having a conventional value, beings exist only in Brahman's self-consciousness & individual personality & ego-sense are only symbols & terms in the universal symbol-existence. We have said that & we shall see that we are not compelled by this perception to set down the world as a myth or a valueless convention. Nor would the Mayavadin himself have been brought to this extreme conclusion if he had not brought into the purity of this highest soul-experience his two other perceptions. The second of these, the lowest, is the perception of the lower or Apara Maya which I have indicated in the opening of this essay — the perception of the system of false values put by mind & sense on the symbol facts of the universe. At a certain stage of our mental culture it is easy to see that the senses are deceiving guides, all mental opinions & judgments uncertain, partial & haunted & pursued by doubt, the world not a reality in the sense in which the mind takes it for a reality, in the sense in which the senses only occupied by & only careful of the practical values of things, their vyavaharic artha, deal with it as a reality. Reaching this stage the mind arrives at this perception that all its values for the world being false, perhaps it is because there is no true value or only a true value not conceivable to the mind, and from this idea it is easy for our impatient human nature to stride to the conclusion that so it is & all existence or all world-existence at least is illusory, a sensation born of nothingness, a play of zeros. Hence Buddhism, the sensational Agnostic philosophies, Mayavada. Again, it is easy at a certain stage of moral culture to perceive that the moral values put by the emotions, passions and aspirations on actions & experiences are false values, that the objects of our sins are not worth sinning for & even that our principles & values do not stand in the shock of the world's actualities, but are, they too, conventional values which we do not find to be binding on the great march of Nature. From this it is natural & right to come to vairagya or dissatisfaction with a life of false valuations and very easy to stride forward, again in the impatience of our imperfect human nature, to the consummation of an entire vairagya, not only dissatisfaction with a false moral life, but disgust with life of any sort & the conclusion of the vanity of world-existence. We have a mental vairagya, a moral vairagya and to these powerful motives is added in the greater types the most powerful of all, spiritual vairagya. For at a certain stage of spiritual culture we come to the perception of the world as a system of mere consciousness values in Parabrahman or to a middle term, the experience, which was probably the decisive factor in the minds of great spiritual seekers like Shankara, of the pure & bright impersonal Sachchidananda beyond, unaffected by & apparently remote from all cosmic existence. Observing intellectually through the mind this great experience, the conclusion is natural & almost inevitable that this Pure & Bright One regards the universe as a mirage, an unreality, a dream. But these are only the terms, the word-values & conventional idea-values into which mind then translates this fact of unaffected transcendence; & it so translates it because these are the terms it is itself accustomed to apply to anything which is beyond it, remote from it, not practically affecting it in tangible relations. The mind engrossed in matter at first accepts only an objective reality; everything not objectivised or apparently capable of some objective expression it calls a lie, a mirage, a dream, an unreality or, if it is favourably disposed an ideal. When, afterwards, it corrects its views, the first thing it does is to reverse its values; coming into a region & level where life in the material world seems remote, unspiritual or apparently not capable of spiritual realisation, it immediately applies here its old expressions dream, mirage, lie, unreality or mere false idea and transfers from object to spirit its exclusive & intolerant use of the word-symbol reality. Add to this mental translation into its own conventional word-values of the fact of unaffected transcendence the intellectual conclusions & temperamental repulsions of mental & moral vairagya, both together affecting & disfiguring the idea of the world as a system of consciousness values and we have Mayavada.

Section Three

The Absolute and the Manifestation

Om Tat Sat

The highest interpretation hitherto made in human understanding and experience may thus be stated with the proviso that since it is human it must be incomplete.

TAT. That.

The Absolute Unmanifested — Parabrahman, Purushottama, Parameswara (holding in himself the Parâshakti and in her the All).

SAT. The Existent (I Am.)

The Absolute containing all the power of the manifestation. The Absolute is Parabrahman-Mahâmâyâ. The Absolute is Purushottama-Parâprakriti. The Absolut is Parameswara-Âdyâ (original) Parâshakti.

OM. The Word of Manifestation.

A The external manifestation (consciousness realised in the actual and concrete — seen by the human consciousness as the waking state.)

U The internal manifestation (intermediate — the inner, not the inmost being — consciousness realised in the inner potentialities and intermediate states between the inmost supramental and the external seen by the human consciousness as the subliminal and associated with the dream state.)

M The inmost seed or condensed consciousness (the inmost supramental, glimpsed by the human consciousness as something superconscient, omniscient and omnipotent, and associated with the state of dreamless Sleep or full Trance.)

AUM Turiya, the Fourth; the pure Spirit beyond these three, Atman consciousness entering into Tat Sat and able to identify with it. Believed to be obtainable in its absoluteness only in absolute Trance — nirvikalpa samadhi.

All this (first in the Upanishads) is the viewpoint from the mental consciousness. It is incomplete because two things that are one have been left out, the Personal Manifestation and the name of the Mahashakti. The subsequent growth of spiritual knowledge has brought about a constant effort to add these missing elements.

When the hidden secret has been discovered and made effective, the human consciousness will be exceeded, the superconscient made conscient and the subconscient or inconscient which is the inevitable shadow of the superconscient filled with the true spiritual and supramental consciousness. The Trance, Dream and Waking States (all imperfect at present and either touched with obscurity or limited) become each completely conscious and the walls, gaps or reversals of consciousness that intervene between them are demolished.

*

Tat then will appear in its entire truth, the Supreme Absolute, One in Two, each entirely in the other and both one in an ineffable Existence, Consciousness and Ananda.

Sat is the eternal and infinite truth of Sachchidananda ready for manifestation. It is the One Existence, but the Two in One are there, each in each, each perfect in the other.

OM is the manifestation. The Mahashakti comes forth from the Supreme for creation. In the eternal manifestation the Two in One are evident to each other; their identity and union are foundation of the diversity of this play, and it is the possession of the truth that makes the manifestation stable & eternal.

In the temporal creation Sat seems to be separated from Chit and Ananda. Hence the play of the inconscience becomes possible and the creation of an Ignorance and an ignorant Maya. The Chit-Shakti has to reveal the Sat Purusha to herself and her creation and entirely to meet him and recover the true identity and union in the Ananda. She seems to be put out from him, but all the time she is in him and he in her. It is this concealed truth that has to become manifest and effective and its discovery is the secret of the new creation in which the superconscient and inconscient will become conscious and fill with the supreme Sacchidananda, One in Two and Two in One. Then the temporal manifestation will be recreated in the image of the Truth. It will be in harmony with the eternal manifestation, built by what comes down to it directly from the Eternal. For through the Ananda and the Supramental the eternal manifestation stands behind the temporal creation and secretly supports its involved and evolving movements.

The Supreme Mahashakti

The secret name of the Supreme Mahashakti signifies

मयोभूः ... राधा	Love, Bliss,	*Ananda*
महामाया, पराप्रकृति	Creative and Formative Knowledge-Power	*Chit-Tapas*
	Support, Covering, Pervasion	*Sat*

For the Supreme is Ananda unifying Consciousness and Existence in the single Power (Shakti) of these things.

*

All is created by the Supreme Goddess, the Supreme and Original Mahashakti, all proceeds from her, all lives by her, all lives in her, even as she lives in all. All wisdom and knowledge are her wisdom and knowledge; all power is her power, all will and force her will and force, all action is her action, all movement her movement. All beings are portions of her power of existence.

*

Seven times seven are the planes of the Supreme Goddess, the steps of ascent and descent of the Divine Transcendent and Universal Adyashakti.

Above are the thrice seven supreme planes of Sat-Chit-Ananda, त्रिः सप्त परमा पदानि मातुः; in between are the seven planes of the Divine Truth and Vastness, Mahad Brahma, सत्यमृतं बृहत्; below are the thrice seven steps of the ascent and descent into this evolutionary world of the earth existence.

These three gradations are successively Supermind or Truth-Mind, with its seven suns; Life with its seven Lotuses; Earth with its seven Jewel-Centres. The seven Lotuses are the seven chakras of the Tantric tradition, descending and ascending from Mind (Sahasradala, Ajna[,] Vishuddha, Anahata) that takes up Life through Life in Force (Manipura, Swadhisthana) down to Life involved in Matter [(]Muladhara[)].

All these Life-Centres are in themselves centres of Truth in Life even as the seven Suns are each a flaming heart of Truth in luminous Divine-Mind-Existence; but these lotuses have been veiled, closed, shut into their own occult energies by the Ignorance. Hence the obscurity, falsehood, death, suffering of our existence.

The Jewel-Centres of the Earth-Mother are seven luminous jewel-hearts of Truth in Substance; but they have been imprisoned in darkness, fossilised in immobility, veiled, closed, shut into their own occult energies by the hardness, darkness and inertia of the material Inconscience.

To liberate all these powers by the luminous and flaming descent of the suns of the Supermind and the release of the eighth Sun of Truth hidden in the Earth, in the darkness of the Inconscience, in the cavern of Vala and his Panis, this is the first step towards the restoration of the Earth Mother to her own divinity and the earth-existence to its native light, truth, life and bliss of immaculate Ananda.

The Seven Suns of the Supermind

1. The Sun of Supramental Truth, — Knowledge-Power originating the supramental creation.
   Descent into the Sahasradala.

2. The Sun of Supramental Light and Will-Power, transmitting the Knowledge Power as dynamic vision and command to create, found and organise the supramental creation.
   Descent into the Ajna-chakra, the centre between the eyes.

3. The Sun of the Supramental Word, embodying the Knowledge-Power, empowered to express and arrange the supramental creation
   Descent into the Throat-Centre.

4. The Sun of supramental Love, Beauty and Bliss, releasing the Soul of the Knowledge-Power to vivify and harmonise the supramental creation.
   Descent into the Heart-Lotus

5. The Sun of Supramental Force dynamised as a power and source of life to support the supramental creation
   Descent into the navel centre

6. The Sun of Life-Radiances (Power-Rays) distributing the dynamis and pouring it into concrete formations.
   Descent into the penultimate centre

7. The Sun of supramental Substance-Energy and Form-Energy empowered to embody the supramental life and stabilise the creation.

   Descent into the Muladhara.

The Seven Centres of the Life

1. The thousand-petalled Lotus — above the head with its base on the brain. Basis or support in Life-Mind for the Supramental; initiative centre of the illumined Mind.

2 The centre between the brows in the middle of the forehead. Will, vision, inner mental formation, active and dynamic Mind.

3 The centre in the throat. Speech, external mind, all external expression and formation.

4 The heart-lotus. Externally, the emotional mind, the vital mental: in the inner heart the psychic centre

5 The navel centre. The larger vital proper; life-force centre.

6 The centre intermediate between the navel and the Muladhara. The lower vital; it connects all the above centres with the physical

7 The last centre or Muladhara. Material support of the vital; initiation of the physical.

All below is the subconscient physical.

SUPREME SELF-CONTAINED ABSOLUTE

–

First Absolute – Tat. The Absolute Transcendent, the Supreme, Paratpara, (containing all, limited by nothing).

Second Absolute – Sat. The supreme self-contained absolute Existence, Sachchidananda, (Ananda uniting Sat & Chit), holding in its absolute unity the dual Principle (He & She, Sa and Sâ) and the fourfold Principle, OM with its four states as one.

Third Absolute – Aditi – M [the Mother]. Aditi is the indivisible consciousness force and Ananda of the Supreme; M, its living dynamis, the supreme Love, Wisdom, Power. Adya-Shakti of the Tantra = Parabrahman

Fourth Absolute – Parameswara of the Gita = Parameswari of the Tantra

=

TAT

|

SAT

|

ADITI - M.

|

PARAMESWARA = PARAMESWARI

→ | ←

↑

THE MANIFESTATION

SUPREME SELF-CONTAINED
ABSOLUTE

First Absolute - Tat. The Absolute Transcendent, the Supreme, Paratpara, (containing all, limited by nothing).

Second Absolute - Sat (combining Sat & Chit). The supreme self-contained absolute Existence, Sachchidananda, holding in its absolute unity the dual Principle (He & She, Sa and Sâ) and the fourfold Principle, OM with its four states as one.

Third Absolute - Aditi-M. Aditi is the indivisible consciousness, force, and Ananda of the Supreme; M holding the dynamic, Love, Wisdom, Power. Adya-Shakti = Parashakti of the Tantra.

Fourth Absolute - Parameswara of the Gita = Parameswari of the Tantra.

TAT
SAT
ADITI - M

PARAMESWARA = PARAMESWARI

THE MANIFESTATION

THE MANIFESTATION

I

First Absolute – The concealed Avyakta Supreme, self-involved Sachchidananda, Parabrahman (Parameswara-iswari)

Second Absolute – Aditi – M. containing in herself the Supreme. The Divine Consciousness, Force, Ananda upholding all the universes – Para Shakti, Para Prakriti, Mahamaya (yayedam dhâryate jagat).

Third Absolute – The Eternal Manifestation (The supreme Satya Loka, Chaitanyaloka, Tapoloka, Ananda-loka – not those of the mental series.)

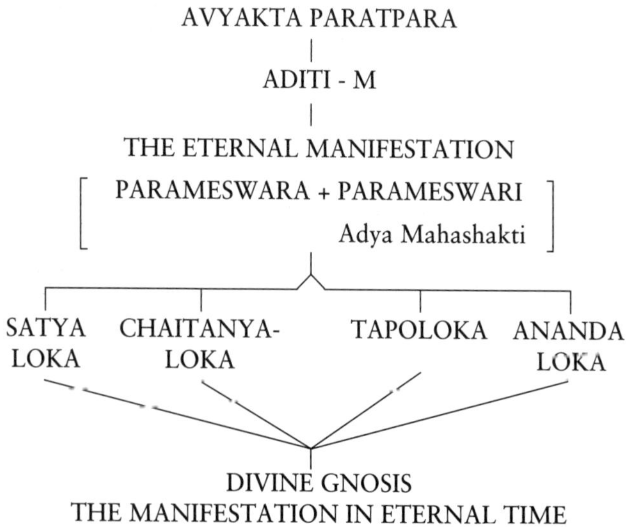

THE MANIFESTATION —

I

First Absolute The concealed Avyakta Supreme, self-involved Sachchidananda, Parabrahman (Paramesvara-Isvara)

Second Absolute — Aditi-M. The Divine Consciousness containing in herself of the Supreme, Force, Ananda upholding all the universes — Para Shakti, Para Prakriti, Mahamaya (yayedam dharyate jagat).

Third Absolute — The Eternal Manifestation (the supreme Satyaloka, Chaitanyaloka, Tapoloka, Ananda-loka — not those of the mental series.)

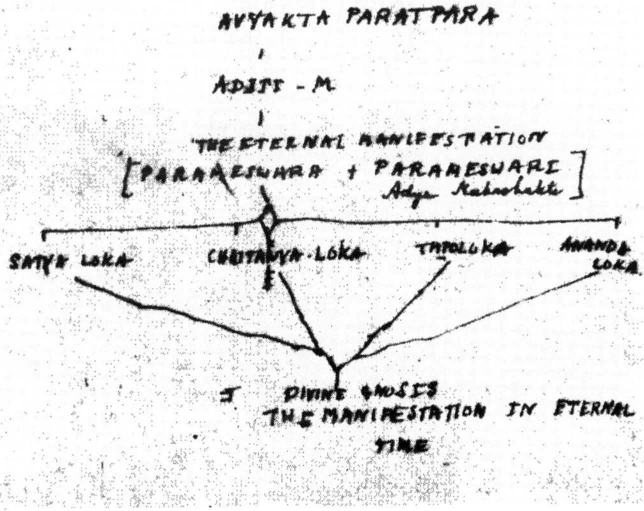

II

The Manifestation in Eternal Time

DIVINE GNOSIS
Satyam Ritam Brihat
=
AVYAKTA PARATPARA
|
ADITI - M
[VIJNANESWARA-VIJNANESWARI]
|

SADGHANA LOKA	CHIDGHANA ◇ TAPOGHANA LOKA	ANANDAGHANA LOKA

The Thrice Seven Supreme Planes of the Mother.
|
VIJNANA LOKA
|
TRUTH-MIND
|
TRUTH-LIFE
|
TRUTH-FORM IN PERPETUAL SUBSTANCE

The Temporal Manifestation

The Manifestation in Eternal Time.

DIVINE GNOSIS

Satyam Ritam Brihat

AVYAKTA PARATPARA

|

ADITI M.

|

[VIJNANESWARA – VIJNANESWARI]

SADGHANA LOKA — CHIDGHANA LOKA (TAPOGHANA) — ANANDAGHANA LOKA

The Three Seven Supreme Planes of the Mother.

|

VIJNANA LOKA

|

TRUTH-MIND

|

TRUTH – LIFE

|

TRUTH – FORM IN SPIRITUAL SUBSTANCE

The Temporal Manifestation

THE SUPREME

|

Sachchidananda – Unmanifest, making possible every kind of manifestation.

|

SACHCHIDANANDA IN MANIFESTATION

The Supreme Planes of Infinite Consciousness

(1) Sat (implying Chit-Tapas and Ananda)

(2) Chit (implying Sat and Ananda)

(3) Ananda (implying Sat and Chit-Tapas.)

|

SUPERMIND or DIVINE GNOSIS.

(The Self-Determining Infinite Consciousness)

From the point of view of our ascent upwards this is the Truth-Consciousness as distinguished from all below that belongs to the separative Ignorance.

|

OVERMIND or MAYA

(Overmind takes all Truth that comes down to it from the Supermind, but sets up each Truth as a separate force and idea capable of conflicting with the others as well as cooperating with them. Each overmental being has his own world, each force has its own play and throws itself out to realise its own fulfilment in the cosmic play. All is possible; and from this separative seat of conflicting and even mutually negating possibilities comes too, as soon as mind, life and matter are thrown out into play[,] the possibility of ignorance, unconsciousness, falsehood, death and suffering.)

—

THE SUPREME

|

Sachchidananda – Unmanifest, making possible every kind of manifestation.

|

SACHCHIDANANDA IN MANIFESTATION

The Supreme Planes of Infinite Consciousness

(1) Sat (implying Chit-Tapas and Ananda)

(2) Chit (implying Sat and Ananda).

(3) Ananda (implying Sat and Chit-Tapas)

|

SUPERMIND or DIVINE GNOSIS.

(The Self-Determining Infinite Consciousness)

From the point of view of our ascent upwards this is the Truth-Consciousness as distinguished from all below that belongs to the separative Ignorance.

|

OVERMIND or MAYA

(Overmind takes all Truth that comes down to it from the Supermind, but sets each Truth as a separate force and idea capable of conflicting with the others as well as cooperating with them. Each being organised has his own world, and from here it can play and strive itself out to realise its own fulfilment in the cosmic play. All is possible; and from this separative sense of conflicting and mutually negating possibilities comes too, as soon as mind, life and matter are thrown out into play, the possibility of ignorance, unconsciousness, falsehood, death and suffering.)

—

OVERMIND GRADATION TO MIND

=

OVERMIND GNOSIS
(Supermind subdued to the overmind play, limited and serving for true but limited creations).

OVERMIND PROPER

Formative Maya (Essential) – Overmind Logos (Determinative of Relations) – Intuitive Overmind (Perceptive of all things created by the two other powers)

HIGHEST MIND
(Intuitive Consciousness)

HIGHER MIND

Illumined

Intuitive

Liberated Intelligence

MIND PROPER (HUMAN)

Thinking Reason

Dynamic Intelligence (Will, Vision etc.) Centre [in][1] the Forehead

Externalising Intelligence (Throat Centre)

Vital Mind

Physical Mind

LOWER CREATION

MIND
VITAL
PHYSICAL

(Vital Mind
Vital Proper
Physical Vital)

[1] *MS* between

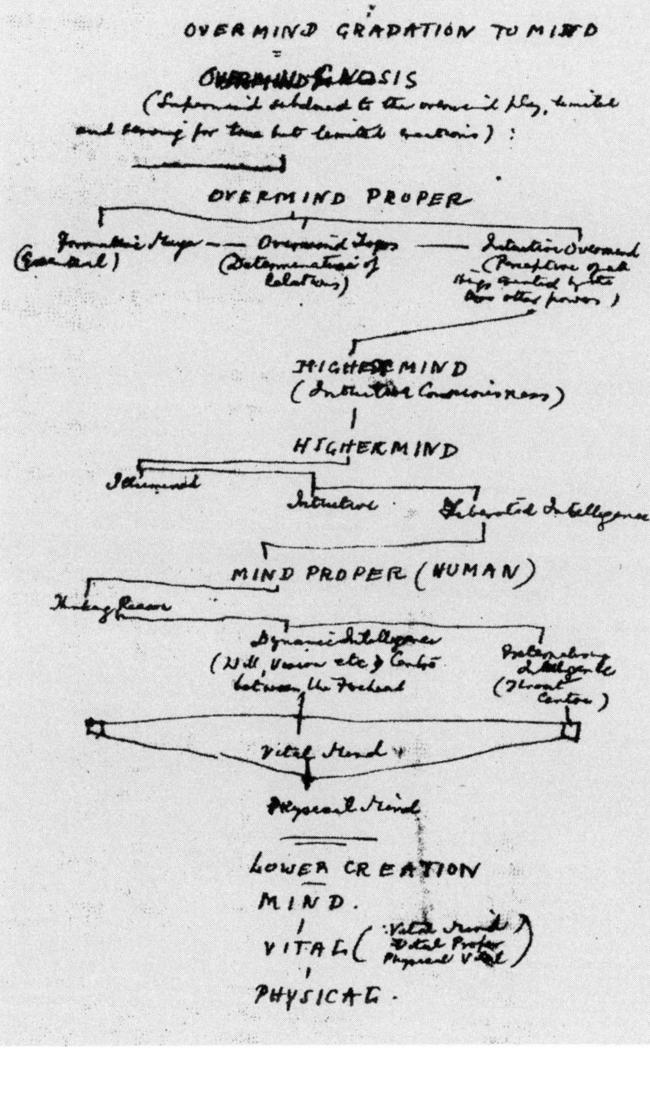
OVERMIND GRADATION TO MIND
=
GNOSIS
(Supermind subdued to the overmind play, limited and serving for time but limitless creations):
OVERMIND PROPER
Formative Maya (Essential)
Overmind Logos (Determinations of Relations)
Intuitive Overmind (Perceptive of all things limited by the three other powers)
HIGHEST MIND
(Intuitive Consciousness)
HIGHER MIND
Illumined
Intuitive
Liberated Intelligence
MIND PROPER (HUMAN)
Thinking Reason
Dynamic Intelligence (Will, Vision etc) Centre between the Forehead
Externalising Intelligence (Throat Centre)
Vital Mind
Physical Mind
LOWER CREATION
MIND.
VITAL (Vital Mind, Vital Proper, Physical Vital)
PHYSICAL.

Section Four

Man and Superman

Man and the Supermind

Man is a transitional being, he is not final; for in him and high beyond him ascend the radiant degrees which climb to a divine supermanhood.

The step from man towards superman is the next approaching achievement in the earth's evolution. There lies our destiny and the liberating key to our aspiring, but troubled and limited human existence — inevitable because it is at once the intention of the inner Spirit and the logic of Nature's process.

The appearance of a human possibility in a material and animal world was the first glint of a coming divine Light, — the first far-off intimation of a godhead to be born out of Matter. The appearance of the superman in the human world will be the fulfilment of that distant shining promise.

The difference between man and superman will be the difference between mind and a consciousness as far beyond it as thinking mind is beyond the consciousness of plant and animal; the differentiating essence of man is mind, the differentiating essence of superman will be supermind or a divine gnosis.

Man is a mind imprisoned, obscured and circumscribed in a precarious and imperfect living but imperfectly conscious body. The superman will be a supramental spirit which will envelop and freely use a conscious body, plastic to spiritual forces. His physical frame will be a firm support and an adequate radiant instrument for the spirit's divine play and work in Matter.

Mind, even free and in its own unmixed and unhampered element, is not the highest possibility of consciousness; for mind is not in possession of Truth, but only a minor vessel or an instrument and here an ignorant seeker plucking eagerly at a mass of falsehoods and half-truths for the unsatisfying pabulum of its hunger. Beyond mind is a supramental or gnostic power of consciousness that is in eternal possession of Truth; all its motion and feeling and sense and outcome are instinct and luminous with the inmost reality of things and express nothing else.

Supermind or gnosis is in its original nature at once and in the same movement an infinite wisdom and an infinite will. At its source it is the dynamic consciousness of the divine Knower and Creator.

When in the process of unfolding of an always greater force of the one Existence, some delegation of this power shall descend into our limited human nature, then and then only can man exceed himself and know divinely and divinely act and create; he will have become at last a conscious portion of the Eternal. The superman will be born, not a magnified mental being, but a supramental power descended here into a new life of the transformed terrestrial body. A gnostic supermanhood is the next distinct and triumphant victory to be won by the spirit descended into earthly nature.

The disk of a secret sun of Power and Joy and Knowledge is emerging out of the material consciousness in which our mind works as a chained slave or a baffled and impotent demiurge; supermind will be the formed body of that radiant effulgence.

Superman is not man climbed to his own natural zenith, not a superior degree of human greatness, knowledge, power, intelligence, will, character, genius, dynamic force, saintliness, love, purity or perfection. Supermind is something beyond mental man and his limits, a greater consciousness than the highest consciousness proper to human nature.

Man is a being from the mental worlds whose mentality works here involved, obscure and degraded in a physical brain, shut off from its own divinest powers and impotent to change life beyond certain narrow and precarious limits. Even in the highest of his kind it is baulked of its luminous possibilities of supreme force and freedom by this dependence. Most often and in most men it is only a servitor, a purveyor of amusements, a caterer of needs and interests to the life and the body. But the superman will be a gnostic king of Nature; supermind in him even in its evolutionary beginnings will appear as a ray of the eternal omniscience and omnipotence. Sovereign and irresistible it will lay hands on the mental and physical instruments, and, standing above and yet penetrating and possessing our lower already manifested parts, it will transform mind, life and body into its own divine and luminous nature.

Man in himself is hardly better than an ambitious nothing. He is a narrowness that reaches towards ungrasped widenesses, a littleness straining towards grandeurs which are beyond him, a dwarf enamoured of the heights. His mind is a darkened ray in the splendours of the universal Mind. His life is a striving exulting and suffering wave, an eager passion-tossed and sorrow-stricken or a blindly and dully toiling petty moment of the universal Life. His body is a labouring perishable speck in the material universe. An immortal soul is somewhere hidden within him and gives out from time to time some sparks of its presence, and an eternal spirit is above and overshadows with its wings and upholds with its power this soul continuity in his nature. But that greater spirit is obstructed from descent by the hard lid of his constructed personality and this inner radiant soul is wrapped, stifled and oppressed in dense outer coatings. In all but a few it is seldom active, in many hardly perceptible. The soul and spirit in man seem rather to exist above and behind his formed nature than to be a part of its visible reality; subliminal in his inner being or superconscient above in some unreached status, they are in his outer consciousness possibilities rather than things realised and present. The spirit is in course of birth rather than born in Matter.

This imperfect being with his hampered, confused, ill-ordered and mostly ineffective consciousness cannot be the end and highest height of the mysterious upward surge of Nature. There is something more that has yet to be brought down from above and is now seen only by broken glimpses through sudden rifts in the giant wall of our limitations. Or else there is something yet to be evolved from below, sleeping under the veil of man's mental consciousness or half visible by flashes, as life once slept in the stone and metal, mind in the plant and reason in the cave of animal memory underlying its imperfect apparatus of emotion and sense-device and instinct. Something there is in us yet unexpressed that has to be delivered by an enveloping illumination from above. A godhead is imprisoned in our depths, one in its being with a greater godhead ready to descend from superhuman summits. In that descent and awakened joining is the secret of our future.

Man's greatness is not in what he is but in what he makes possible. His glory is that he is the closed place and secret workshop of a living labour in which supermanhood is made ready by a divine Craftsman.

But he is admitted to a yet greater greatness and it is this that, unlike the lower creation, he is allowed to be partly the conscious artisan of his divine change. His free assent, his consecrated will and participation are needed that into his body may descend the glory that will replace him. His aspiration is earth's call to the supramental Creator.

If earth calls and the Supreme answers, the hour can be even now for that immense and glorious transformation.

The Involved and Evolving Godhead

The involution of a superconscient Spirit in inconscient Matter is the secret cause of this visible and apparent world. The keyword of the earth's riddle is the gradual evolution of a hidden illimitable consciousness and power out of the seemingly inert yet furiously driven force of insensible Nature. Earth-life is one self-chosen habitation of a great Divinity and his aeonic will is to change it from a blind prison into his splendid mansion and high heaven-reaching temple.

The nature of the Divinity in the world is an enigma to the mind, but to our enlarging consciousness it will appear as a presence simple and inevitable. Freed we shall enter into the immutable stability of an eternal existence that puts on this revealing multitude of significant mutable forms. Illumined we shall become aware of the indivisible light of an infinite consciousness that breaks out here into multiform grouping and detail of knowledge. Sublimated in might, we shall share the illimitable movement of an omnipotent force that works out its marvels in self-imposed limits. Fixed in griefless bliss we shall possess the calm and ecstasy of an immeasurable Delight that creates for ever the multitudinous waves and rhythms and the ever increasing outward-going and inward-drawing intensities of its own creative and communicative world possessing and self-possessing bliss. This, since we are inwardly souls of that Spirit, will be the nature of our fourfold experience when the evolving Godhead will work here in its own unveiled movement.

If that full manifestation had been from the beginning, there would be no terrestrial problem, no anguish of growth, no baffled seeking out of mind and will and life and body towards knowledge and force and joy and an immortal persistence. But this Godhead, whether within us or outside in things and forces and creatures, started from an involution in inconscience of Nature and began by the manifestation of its apparent opposites. Out of a vast cosmic inconscience and inertia and insensibility, an initial disguise that is almost non-existence, the Spirit in Matter has chosen to evolve and slowly shape, as if in a grudging and gradually yielding material, its might and light and infinity and beatitude.

The significance of the terrestrial evolution lies in this slow and progressive liberation of some latent indwelling Spirit. The heart of its mystery is the difficult appearance, the tardy becoming of a divine Something or Someone already involved in physical Nature. The Spirit is there with all its potential forces in a first formal basis of its own supporting, yet resistant substance. Its greater subsequent and deliberately emerging movements, life and mind and intuition and soul and supermind and the light of the Godhead are already there, locked up and obscurely compressed into the initial power and first expressive values of Matter.

Before there could be any evolution, there must needs be this involution of the Divine All that is to emerge. Otherwise there would have been not an ordered and significant evolution, but a successive creation of things unforeseeable, not contained in their antecedents, not their inevitable consequences or right followers in sequence.

This world is not an apparent order fortuitously managed by an inexplicable Chance. Neither is it a marvellous mechanism miraculously contrived by a stumblingly fortunate unconscious Force or mechanical Necessity. It is not even a structure built according to his fancy or will by an external and therefore necessarily a limited Creator. Mentally conceivable, each of these solutions can explain one side or appearance of things; but it is a greater truth that can alone successfully join all the aspects and illumine all the facts of the enigma.

If all were indeed a result of cosmic Chance, there would be no necessity of a new advance; nothing beyond mind need appear in the material world, — as indeed there was then no necessity for even mind to arise at all out of the meaningless blind material whirl. Consciousness itself would be only a fortuitous apparition, a strange hallucinating reflection or ghost of Matter.

Or if all were the work of a mechanical Force, then too mind need not have appeared at all as part of the huge grinding engine; there was no indispensable call for this subtler and yet less competent groping mechanic contrivance. No frail thinking brain should have been there to labour over the quite sufficient cogs and springs and pistons of the first unerring machine. A supermind added on this brilliant and painful complication would be still more a superfluity and a luminous insolence; it could be nothing more than a false pretension of transitory consciousness to govern and possess the greater inconscient Force that is its creator.

Or if an experimenting, external and therefore limited Creator were the inventor of the animal's suffering life and man's fumbling mind and this huge mainly unused and useless universe, there was no reason why he should not have stopped short with the construction of a mental intelligence in his creatures, content with the difficult ingenuity of his labour. Even if he were all-powerful and all-wise, he might well pause there, — for if he went farther, the creature would be in danger of rising too near to the level of his Maker.

But if this is the truth of things that an infinite Spirit, an eternal Divine Presence and Consciousness and Force and Bliss is involved and hidden here and slowly emerges, then is it inevitable that its powers or the ascending degrees of its one power should emerge too one after the other till the whole glory is manifested, a mighty divine Fact embodied and dynamic and visible.

All mental ideas of the nature of things, are inconclusive considerations of our insufficient logical reason when it attempts in its limited light and ignorant self-sufficiency to weigh the logical probabilities of a universal order which after all its speculation and discovery must remain obscure to it still and an enigma. The true witness and discoverer is our growing consciousness; for that consciousness is itself the sign and power of the evolving Divine, and its growth out of the apparent inconscience of the material universe is the fundamental, the one abiding, progressive index event of the long earth-story.

Only when this evolving consciousness can grow into its own full divine power will we directly know ourselves and the world instead of catching at tags and tail ends of an insufficient figure of knowledge. This full power of the consciousness is supermind or gnosis, — supermind because to reach it we have to pass beyond and turn upon mind as the mind itself has passed and turned upon life and inconscient matter and gnosis because it is eternally self-possessed of Truth and in its very stuff and nature it is dynamic substance of knowledge.

The true knowledge of things is denied to our reason, because that is not our spirit's greatest essential power but only an expedient, a transitional instrument meant to deal with the appearance of things and their phenomenal process. True knowledge commences only when our consciousness can pass beyond its present normal limit in man: for then it becomes directly aware of its self and of the Power in the world and begins to have at least an initial knowledge by identity which is the sole true knowledge. Henceforward it knows and sees, no longer by the reason groping among external data, but by an ever increasing and always more luminous self-illumining and all illuminating experience. In the end it will become a conscious part of the Divine revealing itself in the world; its life will be a power for the conscious evolution of that which is still unmanifested in the material universe.

The Evolution of Consciousness

All life here is a stage or a circumstance in an unfolding progressive evolution of a Spirit that has involved itself in Matter and is labouring to manifest itself in that reluctant substance. This is the whole secret of earthly existence.

But the key of that secret is not to be found in life itself or in the body; its hieroglyph is not in embryo or organism, — for these are only a physical means or base: the one significant mystery of this universe is the appearance and growth of consciousness in the vast mute unintelligence of Matter. The escape of Consciousness out of an apparent initial Inconscience, — but it was there all the time masked and latent, for the inconscience of Matter is itself only a hooded consciousness — its struggle to find itself, its reaching out to its own inherent completeness, perfection, joy, light, strength, mastery, harmony, freedom, this is the prolonged miracle and yet the natural and all-explaining phenomenon of which we are at once the observers and a part, instrument and vehicle.

A Consciousness, a Being, a Power, a Joy was here from the beginning darkly imprisoned in this apparent denial of itself, this original night, this obscurity and nescience of material Nature. That which is and was for ever, free, perfect, eternal and infinite, That which all is, That which we call God, Brahman, Spirit, has here shut itself up in its own self-created opposite. The Omniscient has plunged itself into Nescience, the All-Conscious into Inconscience, the All-Wise into perpetual Ignorance. The Omnipotent has formulated itself in a vast cosmic self-driven Inertia that by disintegration creates; the Infinite is self-expressed here in a boundless fragmentation; the All-Blissful has put on a huge insensibility out of which it struggles by pain and hunger and desire and sorrow. Elsewhere the Divine is; here in physical life, in this obscure material world, it would seem almost as if the Divine is not but is only becoming, θεος ουχ έστιν αλλα γιγνεται. This gradual becoming of the Divine out of its own phenomenal opposites is the meaning and purpose of the terrestrial evolution.

Evolution in its essence is not the development of a more and more organised body or a more and more efficient life — these are only its machinery and outward circumstance. Evolution is the strife of a Consciousness somnambulised in Matter to wake and be free and find and possess itself and all its possibilities to the very utmost and widest, to the very last and highest. Evolution is the emancipation of a self-revealing Soul secret in Form and Force, the slow becoming of a Godhead, the growth of a Spirit.

In this evolution mental man is not the goal and end, the completing value, the highest last significance; he is too small and imperfect to be the crown of all this travail of Nature. Man is not final, but a middle term only, a transitional being, an instrumental intermediate creature.

This character of evolution and this mediary position

of man are not at first apparent; for to the outward eye it would seem as if evolution, the physical evolution at least were finished long ago leaving man behind as its poor best result and no new beings or superior creations were to be expected any longer. But this appears to us only so long as we look at forms and outsides only and not at the inner significances of the whole process. Matter, body, life even are the first terms necessary for the work that had to be done. New living forms may no longer be appearing freely, but this is because it is not, or at least it is not primarily, new living forms that the Force of evolution is now busied with evolving, but new powers of consciousness. When Nature, the Divine Power, had formed a body erect and empowered to think, to devise, to inquire into itself and things and work consciously both on things and self, she had what she wanted for her secret aim; relegating all else to the sphere of secondary movements, she turned toward that long-hidden aim her main highest forces. For all till then was a long strenuously slow preparation; but throughout it the development of consciousness in which the appearance of man was the crucial turning point had been kept wrapped within her as her ultimate business and true purpose.

This slow preparation of Nature covered immense aeons of time and infinities of space in which they appeared to be her only business; the real business strikes on our view at least when we look with the outward eye of reason as if it came only as a fortuitous accident, in or near the end, for a span of time and in a speck and hardly noticeable corner of one of the smallest provinces of a possibly minor universe among these many boundless finites, these countless universes. If it were so, we could still reply that time and space matter not to the Infinite and Eternal; it is not a waste of labour for That — as it would be for our brief death-driven existences — to work for trillions of years in order to flower only for a moment. But that paradox too is only an appearance — for the history of this single earth is not all the story of evolution — other earths there are even now elsewhere, and even here many earth-cycles came before us, and many are those that will come hereafter.

Nature laboured for innumerable millions of years to create a material universe of flaming suns and systems; for a lesser but still interminable series of millions she stooped to make this earth a habitable planet. For all that incalculable time she was or seemed busy only with the evolution of Matter; life and mind were kept secret in an apparent non-existence. But the time came when life could manifest, a vibration in the metal, a growing and seeking, a drawing in and a feeling outward in the plant, an instinctive force and sense, a nexus of joy and pain and hunger and emotion and fear and struggle in the animal, — a first organised consciousness, the beginning of the long-planned miracle. Thenceforward she was busy no more exclusively with matter for its own sake, but most with palpitant plasmic matter useful for the expression of life; the evolution of life was now her one intent purpose. And slowly too mind manifested in life, an intensely feeling, a crude thinking and planning vital mind in the animal, but in man the full organisation and apparatus, the developing if yet imperfect mental being, the Manu, the thinking, devising, aspiring, already self-conscient creature. And from that time onward the growth of mind rather than any radical change of life became her shining preoccupation, her wonderful wager. Body appeared to evolve no more; life itself evolved little or only so much in its cycles as would serve to express Mind heightening and widening itself in the living body; an unseen internal evolution was now Nature's great passion and purpose.

And if Mind were all that consciousness could achieve, if Mind were the secret Godhead, if there were nothing higher, larger, [no] more miraculous ranges, man could be left to fulfil mind and complete his own being and there would or need be nothing here beyond him, carrying consciousness to its summits, extending it to its unwalled vastnesses, plunging with it into depths unfathomable; he would by perfecting himself consummate Nature. Evolution would end in a Man-God, crown of the earthly cycles.

But Mind is not all; for beyond mind is a greater consciousness; there is a supermind and spirit. As Nature laboured in the animal, the vital being, till she could manifest out of him man, the Manu, the thinker, so she is labouring in man, the mental being till she can manifest out of him a spiritual and supramental godhead, the truth conscious Seer, the knower by identity, the embodied Transcendental and Universal in the individual nature.

From the clod and metal to the plant, from the plant to the animal, from the animal to man, so much has she completed of her journey; a huge stretch or a stupendous leap still remains before her. As from matter to life, from life to mind, so now she must pass from mind to supermind, from man to superman; this is the gulf that she has to bridge, the supreme miracle that she has to perform before she can rest from her struggle and discontent and stand in the radiance of that supreme consciousness, glorified, transmuted, satisfied with her labour.

The subhuman was once here supreme in her, the human replacing it walks now in the front of Time, but still, aim and goal of the future there waits the supramental, the superman, an unborn glory yet unachieved before her.

The Path

The supramental Yoga is at once an ascent towards God and a descent of Godhead into the embodied nature.

The ascent can only be achieved by a one-centred all-gathering upward aspiration of the soul and mind and life and body; the descent can only come by a call of the whole being towards the infinite and eternal Divine. If this call and this aspiration are there, or if by any means they can be born and grow constantly and seize all the nature, then and then only a supramental uplifting and transformation becomes possible.

The call and the aspiration are only first conditions; there must be along with them and brought by their effective intensity an opening of all the being to the Divine and a total surrender.

This opening is a throwing wide of all the nature on all its levels and in all its parts to receive into itself without limits the greater divine Consciousness which is there already above and behind and englobing this mortal half-conscious existence. In the receiving there must be no inability to contain, no breaking down of anything in the system, mind or life or nerve or body under the transmuting stress. There must be an endless receptivity, an always increasing capacity to bear an ever stronger and more and more insistent action of the divine Force. Otherwise nothing great and permanent can be done; the Yoga will end in a break-down or an inert stoppage or a stultifying or a disastrous arrest in a process which must be absolute and integral if it is not [to] be a failure.

But since no human system has this endless receptivity and unfailing capacity, the supramental Yoga can succeed only if the Divine Force as it descends increases the personal power and equates the strength that receives with the Force that enters from above to work in the nature. This is only possible if there is on our part a progressive surrender of the being into the hands of the Divine; there must be a complete and never failing assent, a courageous willingness to let the Divine Power do with us whatever is needed for the work that has to be done.

Man cannot by his own effort make himself more than man; the mental being cannot by his own unaided force change himself into a supramental spirit. A descent of the Divine Nature can alone divinise the human receptacle.

For the powers of our mind, life and body are bound to their own limitations and, however high they may rise or however widely expand, they cannot rise above their natural ultimate limits or expand beyond them. But, still, mental man can open to what is beyond him and call down a supramental Light, Truth and Power to work in him and do what the mind cannot do. If mind cannot by effort become what is beyond mind, supermind can descend and transform mind into its own substance.

If the supramental Power is allowed by man's discerning assent and vigilant surrender to act according to its own profound and subtle insight and flexible potency, it will bring about slowly or swiftly a divine transformation of our present semiperfect nature.

This descent, this working is not without its possibility of calamitous fall and danger. If the human mind or the vital desire seizes hold on the descending force and tries to use it according to its own limited and erring ideas or flawed and egoistic impulses, — and this is inevitable in some degree until this lower mortal has learned something of the way of that greater immortal nature, — stumblings and deviations, hard and seemingly insuperable obstacles and wounds and suffering cannot be escaped and even death or utter downfall are not impossible. Only when the conscious integral surrender to the Divine has been learned by mind and life and body, can the way of the Yoga become easy, straight, swift and safe.

And it must be a surrender and an opening to the Divine alone and to no other. For it is possible for an obscure mind or an impure life force in us to surrender to undivine and hostile forces and even to mistake them for the Divine. There can be no more calamitous error. Therefore our surrender must be no blind and inert passivity to all influences or any influence, but sincere, conscious, vigilant, pointed to the One and the Highest alone.

Self-surrender to the divine and infinite Mother, however difficult, remains our only effective means and our sole abiding refuge. Self-surrender to her means that our nature must be an instrument in her hands, the soul a child in the arms of the Mother.

Notes on the Texts

The pieces collected together in this book were written by Sri Aurobindo between 1910 and 1940. None of them were published during his lifetime; none received the final revision he gave to his major works. Most of the pieces were first printed in various journals published by the Ashram, and subsequently in the different editions of *The Hour of God*, beginning with the first edition (1959).

The essays and diagrams published here are only a selection from the many prose writings produced by Sri Aurobindo at Pondicherry between 1910 and 1950. Those chosen for inclusion are the most complete, fully developed, and clear of his later, posthumously published prose writings.

The pieces collected here were of course never intended by Sri Aurobindo to be parts of a single work. A number were written in groups of two, three or four, but several are separate essays with no textual, as opposed to thematic, relationship to any others. The selection and arrangement of the pieces is the work of the editors.

Three factors have been considered in making the arrangement — physical (manuscript) relation, thematic and stylistic relation, and chronology. Pieces written together in a single notebook have been printed together in the same order as they appear in that notebook. As in previous editions of *The Hour of God*, essays have been grouped in thematic categories — Yoga; Man and Superman (Evolution); etc. These categories are rather consistent chronologically — sufficiently to allow making all but the first section represent a single chronological period, and to permit the arrangement of all the sections except the first in the natural order of earliest to latest.

SECTION ONE: THE HOUR OF GOD

The three essays in this section have been placed together because their subject-matter and style make them suitable opening pieces. They have no physical relation, one not even being from the same period as the others, but they have great similarity in tone, and share the use of the second person singular to address the reader.

The Hour of God. This essay was in all likelihood written in 1918, and not, at any rate, more than a year or two earlier or later. An incomplete text was published as an Ashram "darshan message" in August 1954. The complete text first came out in the November 1979 issue of the *Bulletin of Sri Aurobindo International Centre of Education.*

The Law of the Way. This essay was written in or about 1927, and was first published in the *Bulletin* in April 1951. The manuscript is untitled; the editors have used a phrase from the last sentence as heading. In previous editions the essay was called "The Way".

The Divine Superman. Written in, or shortly after, the

year 1918 (like "The Hour of God"), this essay may have been intended for use in Sri Aurobindo's monthly review *Arya*, which was being published at that time. The essay's first appearance in print, however, was in the *Bulletin* of April 1951.

SECTION TWO: ON YOGA

These nine essays, related in theme, form a neat chronological group: all were written in or about the year 1913.

Certitudes. It is not possible to establish a sure date for this essay, but it was clearly written during the first years of Sri Aurobindo's stay at Pondicherry, i.e. 1910-1914. The range of years might safely be narrowed down to 1911-1913. It was first published in *The Advent* in February 1957. The Sanskrit phrase at the end, a citation from the Bhagavad Gita (4.11), means "as men approach Me, so I accept them to My love" (Sri Aurobindo's translation).

Initial Definitions and Descriptions. The notebook in which this essay was written, probably in 1913, has two titles: "Hints on Yoga" and "The Psychology of Yoga". "Initial Definitions and Descriptions" is the only piece in the notebook that is at all fully developed. It was first published in *The Advent* in November 1951. In the first edition of *The Hour of God* (1959), it was combined with other pieces from the same notebook and pieces from other notebooks under the title "The Web of

Yoga". "Initial Definitions and Descriptions" and "The Object of Our Yoga" (the next piece) are the only parts of "The Web of Yoga" published in the present edition.

The Object of Our Yoga. This essay was found in the same notebook as contains the next two pieces. It was written after them, but probably in the same year, 1913. The essay, untitled in manuscript, was published as part of "The Web of Yoga" in the first edition of *The Hour of God*.

The Entire Purpose of Yoga. Parabrahman, Mukti and Human Thought-Systems. These two essays were written together in this order almost certainly in the year 1913. In manuscript they are headed by the titles given here and the numbers "I" and "II". A third untitled and not fully developed essay, which has been excluded from the present edition, immediately follows them in the same notebook. The three essays were first published in *The Advent* in April 1954 under the editorial title "Purna Yoga".

The Evolutionary Aim in Yoga. The Fullness of Yoga — In Condition. Nature. Maya. These four essays were written probably in 1913 in this order in a single notebook. On the notebook's cover is written "Natural and Supernatural Man"; this was evidently intended to be the general title of a book that would have included these and other pieces. Texts of the four essays first appeared in the April 1981 issue of *Sri Aurobindo: Archives and Research*. A draft of the first essay was published in the first edition of *The Hour of God* (1959) as the first part of Section V of "The Web of Yoga". The second part of this draft, from the phrase "Yoga practised may be in its aim either perfect or partial" to the end, was rewritten by Sri Aurobindo as the second of the four essays published here, "The Fullness of Yoga — In Condition". In this essay the draft is followed rather closely for two and a half paragraphs; after this point the draft is developed on one line and the essay on another. (The significance of the phrase "in condition" in the title is not made clear in the essay; but it is brought out sufficiently well in the draft. See *Sri Aurobindo: Archives and Research*, Vol. 6 (1982), p. 173.) It is likely that no earlier drafts of "Nature" and "Maya" were written; at any rate none were found along with the drafts of the two other pieces. After the opening or, more likely, the whole of "Nature" had been written, Sri Aurobindo returned upon it for revision. At this time he added at the top of the first page of the manuscript the lines that have been printed here as a footnote hanging from the second sentence. Sri Aurobindo seems to have intended these lines to be a new opening for the piece, but since he did not alter the original first sentence to follow the new opening, and since this sentence links "Nature" with the essay that precedes it, the original opening has been retained. "Nature" was at one point to be entitled "Maya, Lila, Prakriti, Chit-Shakti". Individual essays on each of these aspects of the force called Nature were apparently planned, but only "Maya" was written. In the second paragraph of this essay Sri Aurobindo writes of his intention to "look at the Cosmos from ... the standpoint of ... Lila". Although never able to complete an essay on this theme, he did sketch, in two sentences written on the back cover of the notebook, his view on the subject. These sentences are given as a footnote.

SECTION THREE: THE ABSOLUTE AND THE MANIFESTATION

All of these pieces were written in 1926 or 1927, except the last two diagrams, which are from a later period. All of the earlier pieces except one occur in a single notebook.

Om Tat Sat. These three words, written by Sri Aurobindo at the top of this piece, may not have been intended as a title properly speaking. The piece was first published in the *Bulletin* in April 1976.

The Supreme Mahashakti. Under this title the editors have placed three related pieces written on the same general subject in the same notebook in the sequence given. Since, however, unrelated material not published here intervenes between one piece and another, the three pieces have been separated by asterisks. The last two pieces were published in the *Bulletin* in April 1976; the first appears here for the first time.

The theme of the first piece is alluded to in "Om Tat Sat". The Sanskrit words written in *devanāgarī* script transliterate as follows:

mayobhuḥ... rādhā
mahāmāyā, parāprakṛti

The first word is a Vedic epithet meaning "that creates

bliss". *Rādhā* is "the personification of the absolute love for the Divine" (*Letters on Yoga*, p. 796). The last two terms are defined in the glossary of the present volume. Sri Aurobindo may have intended to write a third set of Sanskrit words, but never did.

In the third piece, the two Sanskrit phrases written in *devanāgarī* script transliterate: *satyam ṛtaṁ bṛhat*, and *triḥ sapta paramā padāni mātuḥ*. The first phrase is defined in the glossary; the second means "the thrice seven supreme planes (literally, "footsteps") of the Mother".

The Seven Suns of the Supermind. The version of this piece printed here is the third of three drafts found in the same notebook. It appeared in the first edition of *The Hour of God* (1959).

The Seven Centres of the Life. This piece was written at the same time as those that precede and follow it, but on a separate sheet of paper. It was first published in the *Bulletin* in April 1976.

Supreme Self-Contained Absolute. The Manifestation. The first of these may not be a title, but simply the term written at the top of the diagram. The two pieces were first published in *Mother India* in December 1953 under the editorial title "The Divine Plan".

The Scale of Consciousness. Overmind Gradations to Mind. These diagrams date from 1931. They were intended to be part of a letter sent in reply to a query of one of Sri Aurobindo's disciples, who had asked about certain "systems of spiritual and occult knowledge" each of which "constructs its own schema". These two quoted phrases are taken from the reply finally sent by

Sri Aurobindo to the disciple (published in *Letters on Yoga*, pp. 249-51). Sri Aurobindo's diagrams were never sent; they were published along with the above two diagrams under the same editorial title in the 1959 edition of *The Hour of God*. The Mother has stated in one of her conversations that Sri Aurobindo made these diagrams in a half-playful mood.

SECTION FOUR: MAN AND SUPERMAN

Early drafts of the first two of these essays may be dated with some certainty to 1927. The versions printed here are from a single notebook and may have been written as late as the early 1930s. The other two essays are from the same general period.

Man and the Supermind. There are numerous drafts of this essay and of essays thematically related to it. The first draft is clearly from 1927 or thereabouts. The second, rewritten directly from the first and not long after, was published, with some related passages, under the title "Man A Transitional Being" in the *Bulletin* in August 1951. One more draft intervenes between this and the draft printed in the present volume, which seems to have been written in the early 1930s. It was not published until August 1976, in the *Bulletin*.

The Involved and Evolving Godhead. An earlier draft of this piece, written around 1927, was first published under the title "Evolution" (III) in the *Bulletin* in November 1951. The present draft, written probably during the early 1930s (in the same notebook as "Man and the Supermind"), was first published in the *Bulletin* in August 1976.

The Evolution of Consciousness. This essay was written in the same notebook as the above two pieces, and at about the same time, i.e. around 1930. It was first published in the *Bulletin* in November 1976 as the first of two separate pieces under the title "Evolution". In the present volume the essay, untitled in manuscript, has been headed "The Evolution of Consciousness". The Greek phrase on page 112 means "God is not but is becoming".

The Path. This essay is one of several pieces written around 1930 on the supramental Yoga. Three of these were published together under the editorial title "The Supramental Yoga" in *The Advent* in November 1955. The present piece, the most completely developed of them, is the only one that has a title in the manuscript.

EDITIONS OF *THE HOUR OF GOD*

In 1959 many of the pieces described above, along with others not included in the present edition, were collected together and published under the title *The Hour of God*. A second impression of this edition was issued in 1964. A second edition was brought out in 1970. (It is not possible to determine with certainty whether 1964 was recomposed or not, i.e. whether it was an impression or edition. At any rate both 1964 and 1970 are textually identical to the first edition.) In 1972 all the pieces in

The Hour of God, slightly reorganised, were included in *The Hour of God and Other Writings*, Volume 17 of the Sri Aurobindo Birth Centenary Library. In 1973, the 1972 texts were reproduced photographically in the old order (but with one omission) as the third edition of *The Hour of God*. The fourth edition (1982) was thoroughly reorganised: several pieces included in the first three editions were replaced by later versions of the same pieces, some pieces were omitted entirely, and some others were added. Six impressions of the fourth edition were printed between 1982 and 2002. The present (fifth) edition has the same contents as the fourth. The texts are taken from two volumes of the Complete Works of Sri Aurobindo: volume 12, *Essays in Philosophy and Yoga* (1997) and volume 11, *Record of Yoga–II* (2001).

Glossary of Sanskrit Terms

Most Sanskrit words and phrases occurring in this book are defined below. All words are transliterated according to the international system; where this transliteration differs significantly from the easier (English-orthographic) transliteration sometimes used by Sri Aurobindo, the easier spelling is given within parentheses and a cross-reference is provided.

For Sanskrit words written in *devanāgarī* script see Notes on the Texts under the text concerned.

adhama – lowest.

aditi – the Mother of the Gods; the indivisible consciousness-force of the Supreme; supreme Nature or infinite consciousness.

advaitin (Adwaitin) – a Vedantic Monist.

ādyā mahāśakti – the original *mahāśakti*.

ādyā śakti – original Power; the transcendent Mother.

ahaṁkāra – ego-sense; the divisional principle of ego-formation.

ājñā-cakra – the centre (*cakra*) between the eyebrows, which governs the dynamic mind, will, vision, mental formation.

amṛtam – Immortality.

anāhata – the heart-lotus, the centre (*cakra*) that governs the emotional mind and vital mental.

ānanda – bliss, delight, beatitude, spiritual ecstasy; the essential principle of delight; a self-delight which is the very nature of the transcendent and infinite existence.

ānandaghanaloka – world of dense bliss.

ānandaloka – world of bliss.

annam – matter.

aparā māyā – the lower *māyā*.

aparārdha – the lower hemisphere (of world-existence).

asat – Non-Being; Non-Existence; Nothingness.

ātman – Self; Spirit; the original and essential nature of our existence.

AUM – see *oṁ*.

avatāra – descent (of God in man); Incarnation.

avidyā – the Ignorance; the relative and multiple consciousness.

avyākṛta prakṛti (Avyakrita Prakriti) – undifferentiated Nature.

avyakta – unmanifest.

avyakta parātpara – the unmanifest supreme of the Supreme.

ayodhyā (Ayodhya) – kingdom ruled by Dasharatha and later by his son Rama.

bhūr – the material world.

bhuvar – world of pure vitality.

brahman – the Reality; the Eternal; the Absolute; the Spirit; the One besides whom there is nothing else existent.

caitanyaloka – world of consciousness.

cakra (Chakra) – subtle centre; ganglionic centre in the nervous system.

cid-ātman (Chid-Atman) – Self of consciousness.
cidghanaloka (Chidghanaloka) – world of dense consciousness.
cit (Chit) – consciousness; the principle of pure consciousness.
cit-śakti (Chit-Shakti) – consciousness-force; the divine Energy.
cit-tapas (Chit-Tapas) – consciousness-force; pure energy of consciousness.
dharma – law of being.
eṣa supteṣu jāgarti – this that wakes in the sleepers. (Katha Upanishad 2.2.8)
gati – status of soul-nature; final status of becoming.
guru – teacher; spiritual teacher; guide.
īśvarī – she who has mastery; ruling Mother.
jana – the delight that gives birth to life and world; the world of creative delight of existence (in this sense *janaloka*).
jivanmukta – living liberated man.
jivanmukti – liberation while living.
jñāna-śakti (Jnana-Shakti) – power of knowledge.
kālī – the divine Mother in her terrible aspect as the destroyer of the demons.
kriyā-śakti (Kriya-Shakti) – power of process and action.
kṛṣṇa (Krishna) – the lord of *ānanda*, love and *bhakti* (devotion).
kuvera – the god of riches.
lankā (Lanca) – island kingdom of Ravana, chief of the demons, where he held Sita after abducting her.

līlā (Lila) – play, game; the cosmic play.

līlāmaya – playful; made up of the cosmic play (*līlā*).

madhyama – middle.

mahad brahma – the great *brahman*, the Divine Truth and Vastness.

mahāmāyā – the great *māyā*.

mahar, *mahas* – the great world, the world of Truth; the supramental.

mahatī vinaṣṭiḥ – a great perdition. (Kena Upanishad 2.5)

mahimānam asya – his greatness.

manas – sense-mind; mind.

maṇipūra – the navel centre (*cakra*); it is the life-force centre, governing the larger vital proper.

manomayaḥ prāṇa-śarīra-netā – the mental Being, leader of the life and body. (Mundaka Upanishad 2.2.8)

manu – mental being.

māyā – signified originally in the Veda the comprehensive and creative knowledge; afterwards taken in its second and derivative sense: cunning, magic, illusion; the cosmic illusion; phenomenal consciousness.

māyāvāda – the doctrine holding that the world is *māyā*, i.e. Illusion.

māyāvādin – one who professes the *māyāvāda*; Illusionist.

mūlādhāra – root vessel or chamber; the physical consciousness centre (*cakra*); it is the material support of the vital and governs the physical down to the subconscient.

nirvikalpa samādhi – absolute trance.

oṁ – the *mantra* or expressive sound symbol of the *brahman* in its four domains from the *turīya* to the external or material plane (i.e. the outward looking, the inward or subtle, and the superconscient causal – each letter A, U, M, indicating one of these three in ascending order and the whole bringing out the fourth state, *turīya*).

oṁ tat sat – *oṁ*, That is the thing that Is.

parabrahman – the supreme *brahman*; the Divine.

parā māyā – Supreme formative power; higher divine Nature.

parameśvara (Parameshwara) – supreme Lord.

parameśvarī (Parameshwari) – the supreme *īśvarī*.

parā prakṛti (Para Prakriti) – the supreme Nature.

para-puruṣa (Parapurusha) – supreme Soul; God.

parā śakti – the supreme power.

parātpara – the supreme of the Supreme.

parātpara brahman – *brahman* higher than the highest.

prajñā prasṛtā purāṇī – Wisdom that went forth from the beginning. (Shwetashwatara Upanishad 4.18)

prakṛti (Prakriti) – Nature; Nature-Soul; executive or working force.

prakṛtiṁ yānti bhūtāni, nigrahaḥ kiṁ kariṣyati – all existences follow their nature and what shall coercing it avail? (Gita 3.33)

prāṇa – the life-force, life; the five *prāṇas*: the five workings of the life-force (in man's body).

pūrṇa yoga – the integral yoga.

puruṣa (Purusha) – Person; Conscious Being; Conscious-Soul; Soul; essential being supporting the play of *prakṛti*.

rāma (Rama) – son of Dasharatha, king of Ayodhya; considered to be an incarnation of Vishnu.

ṛṣi (Rishi) – a seer.

sā – she.

saccidānanda (Sachchidananda) – the Divine Being, a trinity of Existence (*sat*), Consciousness (*cit*) and Delight (*ānanda*).

sadghanaloka – world of dense existence.

saḥ – he.

sahasradala – the highest of the *cakras*, the thousand-petalled lotus; initiative centre of the illumined mind.

śakti (Shakti) – Energy, Force, Strength, Will, Power; the self-existent, self-cognitive, self-effective Power of the Lord.

sama – even; equal.

samrāṭ – all-ruler.

śārdūla – tiger.

śāstra (Shastra) – scripture.

sat – being, existence; the Existent.

sat puruṣa – the pure divine Self; God.

sāttvika (sattwic) – consisting of light and poise and peace.

satyaloka – world of (the highest) truth of being.

satyam – truth; truth of being.

satyam ṛtaṁ bṛhat (Satyam Ritam Brihat) – the Truth, the Right, the Vast.

Shakti – see *śakti*.

Shastra – see *śāstra*.

siddha – perfect; perfected.

siddha puruṣa – a perfect being; the superman.
sītā (Sita) – daughter of king Janaka and wife of Rama.
śreyān svadharmo viguṇaḥ – better is one's own law of works, though in itself faulty... (Gita 3.35)
śūnya – zero; void.
suṣupti – deep sleep; the Sleep-State.
svādhiṣṭhāna – the penultimate centre (*cakra*), located between the navel and the *mulādhāra*; it governs the lower vital.
svar (Swar) – world corresponding to the principle of pure or unobscured mind.
svarāṭ (Swarat) – self-ruler.
tad vā etat – that indeed is this.
tapas – heat, energism; the essential principle of energy.
tapasyā – effort, energism, austerity of the personal will; concentration of the will and energy for any yogic or other high purpose.
tapoghanaloka – world of dense *tapas*.
tapoloka – world of *tapas*; world of infinite Will or conscious force.
tat – That (the Absolute).
turīya – the fourth; the fourth plane of our consciousness; the superconscient.
uttama – highest.
vairāgya – distaste; disgust (with the world).
vibhūti – divine power; a power of God in man, embodied World-Force or human leader.
vijñāna – Pure Idea; the free spiritual or divine intelligence; Gnosis; Supermind.
vijñānaloka – the world of *vijñāna*; the supramental world.

vijñāneśvara (Vijnaneshwara) – the Lord of the *vijñāna*.
vijñāneśvarī (Vijnaneshwari) – the *īśvarī* of the *vijñāna*.
viśuddha – the throat centre (*cakra*); it governs speech, external mind, all external expression and formation.
vyāhṛti – each of the three symbolic words of the *mantra*: (*oṁ*) *bhur bhuvaḥ svaḥ*.
vyāvahārika artha – practical value.
yayedaṁ dhāryate jagat – by which this world is upheld. (Gita 7.5)
yoga – union; the union of the soul with the immortal being and consciousness and delight of the Divine; a methodised effort towards this union and towards self-perfection.
yogaḥ hi prabhavāpyayau – for *yoga* is the beginning and ending of things. (Katha Upanishad 2.3.11)
yogin – one who practises *yoga*, especially one who is established in yogic realisation.